CROMWELL'S PRESS AGENT:
A Critical Biography of Marchamont Nedham, 1620-1678

Joseph Frank

University Press of America

Copyright © 1980 by

University Press of America, Inc.
4720 Boston Way, Lanham, MD 20801

All rights reserved
Printed in the United States of America
ISBN: 0-8191-1193-7 (Case)
0-8191-1194-5 (Perfect)

Library of Congress Catalog Card Number: 80-5637

To my wife Florence, who helped in many ways.

CONTENTS

I	OVERTURE: 1621-1643	1
II	FIRST MOVEMENT: 1643-1646	13
III	SECOND MOVEMENT: 1646-1649	39
IV	THIRD MOVEMENT: 1649-1660	73
V	FOURTH MOVEMENT: 1660-1678	143
VI	CODA	169
	APPENDICES	179
	BIBLIOGRAPHY	191

PREFACE

Marchamont Nedham was born in 1620 and died in 1678. His own life was turbulent, and it coincided with a turbulent period in English history, a period that in retrospect is surprisingly modern. Of all his contemporaries Nedham would probably be best equipped to function and flourish on Madison Avenue or Fleet Street, on Capitol Hill or in Westminster. He was Oliver Cromwell's press agent and, on occasion, spy. For fifteen years he was England's most widely read journalist, first on the side of Parliament, then of the King, then of the Commonwealth and Protectorate. He was also an extremely skilled pamphleteer, and he ended his career writing tracts in support of Charles II. Moreover, from 1645 on he was a successful doctor, and in the 1660's he briefly plunged into medical polemics. In all his roles he made a great deal of money, though surprisingly unmodern is the fact that he made more by his pen than by his scalpel. Finally, he was a close friend of John Milton's. His story is thus of more than antiquarian interest.

My own interest in Nedham, however, has lasted long enough to verge on the antiquarian. I first encountered him in 1948 when I was working on the Levellers. A decade later, while trying to read several thousand early English newspapers, I became almost intimate with him, and in the 1960's we maintained a sporadic friendship as I delved into the mass--and mess--of minor Interregnum poetry. Since 1975, I have been working on getting to know him as well as I can--and this book is the result.

I find him sophisticated, many-faceted, unpredictable. Along with all commentators who bother to mention him, I also find Nedham venal and unprincipled, though not the vicious Vicar of Bray that he was to most of his contemporaries and subsequent historians. During the past thirty years, in addition to writing, teaching, and administering, I have been intermittently involved in politics: not only in the academic pits but in local, state, and occasionally in national arenas. I therefore can appreciate the slings and arrows which Nedham both caught and threw, and I admire, if not always approve, his deft footwork and quick-change artistry. In short, I find him a very congenial subject.

Because of this book's long gestation, I owe much to many. I have worked on Nedham at the British Museum and the Folger and Huntington Libraries, and each has been cooperative and generous. Many people over the years have lent a helping hand. But let me bracket them by specifically thanking only two: first, Douglas Bush, who long ago got me started on seventeenth-century studies with a push so firm and friendly that it has not yet lost its momentum; second, Philip Knachel, the editor of one of Nedham's major tracts, who at the Folger recently acted as a resonant sounding board for some of my ideas.

CHAPTER I

OVERTURE-1620-1643

Arthur Koestler begins his autobiography with his "secular horoscope": the major events of the day of his birth as reported in the following day's London Times.[1] The news on September 5, 1905 suggests, at least with hindsight, that Koestler's life would be marked by danger, commitment, controversy. It also suggests why he might shift his allegiances in an era of violence, ideological rigidities, and revolution.

Marchamont Nedham was born in mid-August 1620.[2] No London Times then existed to report the news of the world, but it is possible to reconstruct a rough secular horoscope for that distant day. With hindsight, such a horoscope also foretells a life marked by danger, commitment, controversy, as well as Nedham's shifts in allegiance in an era of violence, ideological rigidities, and revolution.

The foreign news in a hypothetical London Times would be concerned with the opening stages of the Thirty Years War, a war which was to reduce the population of Central Europe by two-thirds. The first major battle had occurred near Prague late in 1618. By the summer of 1620 the armies of the Counter-Reformation seemed to be moving toward the domination of all of Europe, with the possible exception of France. James I, by his vacillation, offered only token help to the Protestant forces, and actually encouraged Spain and its allies to strike quickly and massively. In August the Hapsburg army crossed the Rhine and within two weeks conquered the key cities of the Protestant German princes. On the day that Nedham was born, the forces of the status quo ante appeared to be invincible.[3]

The domestic news of August 1620 was also foreboding. What was happening in Bohemia and points west underlined, for the English, James's subservience to Spain and the ease with which the suave Spanish Ambassador manipulated him. The king's unpopularity was augmented by non-secret negotiations for the marriage of his son to the Infanta. Parliament had not met for six years, and the King added to the mood of political frustration by frequently and conspicuously theorizing about the unlimited power of the Crown. Despite the fact that the doctrine of the divine right of kings was originally anti-Papal, James's combination of vacillation and loquacity fanned the fires of English anti-Catholicism and stimulated the growth and militancy of a variety of Puritan groups. By the day of Nedham's birth the street crowds in London had become distinctly visible and audible--and potentially powerful.[4]

The economic news of that day could also be viewed as ominous. For eighty years a steady inflation had accelerated upward social mobility and enriched the mercantile class, as well as those landowners who expanded their agricultural output. But inflation had reduced the already low standard of living of hundreds of thousands of tenant farmers; and unemployment and wretchedly low wages added to the frustration and discontent of the thousands who were annually gravitating to London, pushing its population close to 500,000.[5]

Down in a corner of a hypothetical financial page might be a half-column reporting that the Earl of Warwick, as a result of Spanish pressure, had been ordered to surrender his authorization to colonize Guiana, even though in August 1620 a cousin of his was still busy in South America. This Guiana Company was to lead to the formation of the Providence Company at the end of the decade. It, in turn, provided John Pym and his business associates with the economic and political training deftly to manage Parliament in the early 1640's.[6] Next to this story might be an item of shipping news: the Mayflower, on August 5, sailed from Southampton but had to turn back. (A month later it would try again, this time from Plymouth.)

On the editorial page a prescient writer might have commented on the rise of national states, the impact of the new science, the growth of skepticism, the beginnings of modern capitalism--and, possibly, on the clouds of civil war gathering on a distant English horizon. But that would be asking too much for even a hypothetical newspaper. As to any actual newspaper: the first one in English, consisting only of news about the war in Bohemia, appeared in Amsterdam three-and-half months after Nedham's birth.[7]

On August 21, 1620 Nedham was baptized in the small town of Burford, about fifteen miles west of Oxford.[8] The only contemporary news item that might be considered worthy of inclusion in even a county weekly is a letter from the Corporation of Oxford, dated September 25, 1620, to the effect that since the Burgesses of Burford had not paid certain rents, they had no right to certain incomes.[9] Other contemporary records confirm that the Burgesses tried to be moderately independent.[10] The town had a population of about 900 and was relatively prosperous, and at the time of Nedham's birth some of the better houses were being fitted with glass windows.[11] When I visited there in 1973 it gave every impression of having long been a sturdy and attractive village.

Nedham's father, also named Marchamont, was "born of genteel parents in Derbyshire." He matriculated at St. John's College, Oxford in June 1610, and received a B.A. degree from Gloucester Hall in February 1612. He then served as "an attendant on the Lady Eliz. Lucas, sister to John Lord Lucas and wife of Sir Will. Walters of Sarsden near Burford." Nedham's mother, Margery, was the daughter of John Collier. Collier was the "host of the George Inn, then the principal place for the reception of guests in Burford." Nedham senior died in 1621; and Margery the following year married Christopher Glynn, vicar of Burford and master of its free-school.[12]

Nedham's father's connections were with the gentry and nobility. Nedham's maternal grandfather, on the basis of fragmentary records, also was well connected and well off, a figure of importance and respect in Burford.[13] The town was on the expanding main route between London and South Wales, and the George Inn had long prospered.[14] Nedham's step-father, Christopher Glynn, was also prosperous and one of Burford's leading citizens. He was a cautious man, "little more than a creature of the lords of the manor," a role that brought him "comfortable payments" throughout his lengthy life.[15] To what extent Glynn's instinct for self-preservation rubbed off on his step-son cannot be determined. But certainly Nedham's own immediate and local secular horoscope was upper bourgeois and propituous.

Nedham received his early education at the Burford free-school, under the eye and probably hand of his step-father. A day school, not a boarding school, it had been founded in 1571. In 1628, when Nedham was a "petty student," its already satisfactory income was increased.[16] According to Anthony á Wood, the seventeenth-century biographer of Oxford graduates, Glynn perceived his step-son "to have very pregnant parts...and spared not to encourage his forwardness."[17]

Peter Heylen, a prolific Royalist and Anglican with whose life Nedham's both clashed and meshed, graduated in 1613 from Burford and went on to Oxford. Heylyn's contemporary biographer says that he learned much Latin and classical history at Burford.[18] In the late 1650's John Wilmot Earl of Rochester also attended Burford. There is no record that Nedham ever met the Earl, though he may have tried to in the 1670's. But a description of the school in Rochester's day is probably pertinent to Nedham's early education:

> Morning school at six o'clock in the summer and seven in the winter and went on till eleven when the boys went to dinner. They began work again at one o'clock and finished at four, after which they either went to

church or sang psalms and read a chapter of the Bible. Every Sunday they came to the master's house at eight in the morning, and went with him to church. Four times a year the master had to exhort them to give thanks to God and to recite the names of all the Founders and Benefactors which were inscribed on a table in the schoolhouse, and then they sung a psalm.[19]

This regimen might account for Rochester's subsequent lifestyle and poetry, and it may help to explain Nedham's somewhat cynical climb to success.

We know from his subsequent works that Nedham actually learned a great deal of Latin and classical history at Burford, as well as presumably acquiring a solid grounding in European history. He also learned Greek.[20] In 1634 he entered All Soul's College, Oxford, receiving his bachelor's degree on October 24, 1637.[21] For part of these three years his status was that of "chorister." I can find nothing in the charters or records of All Souls' which defines this term. I assume that it had little to do with Nedham's being a vocal member of the choir, but that it meant he received a token stipend. Certainly the step-son of Christopher Glynn was not a "serviente" nor a student dependent on charity.

It is also difficult to ascertain what Nedham learned or how he lived at Oxford. All Souls' during his sojourn was a wealthy college with a relatively high standard of living, and one gets the impression that many of its faculty were more interested in securing their perquisites than in educating their students. It was also the college most concerned with training young men for careers in law.[22] Presumably Nedham lived well, nibbled at the law, perfected his Latin and Greek, increased his knowledge of history, and probably acquired some grounding in chemistry and physiology. Somewhere along the line he learned to write quickly and effectively. There is no evidence that he had any sort of conflict with the High Church tendencies of All Souls' under Gilbert

Sheldon, who became Warden in 1635, nor that he clashed with the meticulous Laudian code, which took effect for the entire University in 1636.

After receiving his degree Nedham spent a short time at St. Mary's College, then took a job as an usher in the Merchant Taylors' School in London.[23] It was a prestiguous institution and its students were strenuously taught Latin and Greek according to the most enlightened methods of the day.[24] Getting a job there was something of an academic plum, though its value may have been temporarily lessened because the school had been shut down as a result of the plague for eighteen months prior to Nedham's arrival.[25] His duties almost certainly involved keeping the younger students in line, as well as functioning as an assistant teacher, probably of Latin, Greek, and history. As at Oxford, he stayed out of trouble, for there is no evidence of any contention between him and the ardent Laudian headmaster, William Staple.[26]

Nedham stayed at Merchant Taylors' less than three years. One of his reasons for leaving was the low pay: in a pamphlet he wrote in 1663 he vigorously argued for higher pay for schoolteachers. Also, he may have felt overworked. A semi-facetious poem of 1645, 'The Scholars [of Merchant Taylors'] Petition for Play-dayes in stead of Holy-dayes,' ends with the statement that it was drawn up by 273 of the students, who begged: "O let not then our Masters be our Jailors."[27]

Wood continues his biography of Nedham: "Upon the change of times, he became an under clerk in Greys Inn, where by virtue of a good legible court hand, he obtained a comfortable subsistence."[28] Wood bases his statement on the testimony of two of Nedham's antagonists in 1645, so it is likely that his proficiency rather than his penmanship got him this comfortable subsistence.[29] The "change of times" is late 1640, when Parliament was finally convened for its lengthy, contentious, and frequently interrupted session. Nedham was moving away from academia toward the center of national action.

He stayed at Gray's Inn until the summer of 1643, when he became one of the editors of Parliament's most aggressive and widely read weekly newspaper. He would not have been chosen for this position if he had not shown himself to be far more than a good legal stenographer. At the age of twenty-three he was about to begin his long and successful career as a journalist and propagandist, and he was beginning it near the top.

This career supplies few intimate glimpses of Nedham. In 1645 a hostile pamphlet describes him as short, thickset, black-haired.[30] Wood, a generation later, writes that "he was a person endowed with quick natural parts, was a good humanitian, poet, and boon droll: and had he been constant to his cavaleering principles he would have been beloved by, and admired of, all; but being very mercenary and valuing money and sordid interest, rather than conscience, friendship, or love to his prince, was much hated by the royal party to his last, and many cannot yet endure to hear him spoken of."[31] Wood again may not be entirely accurate, and the concluding chapter of this book will suggest modification of this generally unpleasant portrait.

Nedham was a very prolific writer and he fleshes out his own portrait-but only as a public figure. What we know about his personal life comes from a few bare official entries. They show that he was married twice: first to a woman named Lucy, by whom, in 1652, he had a son named Marchamont; second, in 1663, to a widow, Elizabeth Thompson.[32] The rest, so far as the private Nedham is concerned, is mainly silence. Not so the public Nedham, whose career from 1643 on was usually very high decibel.

Footnotes   Chapter I

In all quotations in the text and notes I have avoided "sic's": seventeenth-century spelling, which I have retained, is irregular enough to speak for itself. I have usually ignored italics, as sometimes they are haphazard and often they are distracting. I have made extremely few changes in punctuation, and then only for the sake of clarity.

1. Arthur Koestler, Arrow in the Blue, London: Collins 1952.

2. Most of the facts of Nedham's life come from Anthony á Wood, Athenae Oxoniensis, London: Tho. Bennet, 1691, supplemented occasionally by Charles H. Firth's article in The Dictionary of National Biography. Nedham is frequently spelled Needham, and there are a few contemporary variations on Marchamont.

3. For a clear account of these tangled events, see C.V. Wedgwood, The Thirty Years War, London: Jonathan Cape, 1938.

4. For the preliminary background of the English Civil Wars, Samuel Rawson Gardiner's ten-volume History of England from the Accession of James I to the Outbreak of the Civil War, 1603-1642 (London: Longmans, Green, 1895) is indispensable.

5. For further details, see Christopher Hill, The Century of Revolution, 1603-1714, Edinburgh: Thomas Nelson and Sons, Ltd., 1961, pp. 15-42; Valerie Pearl, London and the Outbreak of the Puritan Revolution, London: Oxford University Press, 1961, p. 38.

6. The saga of this training-connecting the Old World and the New, and intermingling the slave trade and Puritan evangelism-is told in Arthur Percival Newton, The Colonizing Activities of

the English Puritans, reprinted Port Washington: Kennikot Press, Inc., 1966.

7. On Dec. 2, 1620: see Joseph Frank, The Beginnings of the English Newspaper, 1620-1660, Cambridge: Harvard University Press, 1961, p. 36 (hereafter referred to as BN).

8. Wood, p. 1180.

9. R.H. Gretton, The Burford Records, Oxford: At the Clarendon Press, 1920, p. 401.

10. Mary Jessup, A History of Oxfordshire, London: Phillimore & Co., Ltd., 1975, p. 57: the reports, between 1617 and 1619, concerning the Burford Burgesses' practice of running the market, collecting tolls, drawing up bylaws, and holding a local court. These activities were challenged, however, by the new lord of the manor, who proceeded to win his case.

11. Gretton, Burford Records, pp. 207ff.; Mary Sturge Gretton, Burford Past and Present, London: Faber and Faber Limited, 1945, p. 23.

12. Wood, p. 1180; Firth, DNB.

13. Gretton, Burford Records, pp. 326, 351, 368.

14. Mary Gretton, Burford, p. 19.

15. Gretton, Burford Records, p. 138. Glynn had sided with the new lord of the manor in his quarrel with the Burgesses (see above, note 10). A later indication of his caution is that at the end of the Leveller mutiny in Burford in 1649, he made a non-committal entry in the church registrar, merely recording "three soldiers shot to death in Burford churchyard buried May 17th" (Mary Gretton, Burford, p. 29.)

16. Mary Gretton, Burford, pp. 58ff.

17. Wood, p. 1180.

18. George Vernon, The Life of Peter Heylyn, London: 1682, p. 5.

19. Vivian de Sola Pinto, Enthusiast in Wit, A Portrait of John Wilmot Earl of Rochester 1647-1680. London: Routledge &. Kegan Paul, 1962, p. 5.

20. In his preface to Edward Bolnest's Medicina Instaurata (1665) Nedham says that he knew Greek by the age of fourteen.

21. Firth, DNB.

22. Charles Mallet, A History of the University of Oxford, New York: Longmans, Green and Co., 1924, I, 362-380, passim. V.H.H. Green, A History of Oxford, London: B.T. Botsford, Ltd., 1974, p. 78, reports on the increasing consumption of wine by students and faculty in the seventeenth century.

23. Wood, p. 1180; Firth, DNB.

24. Philip Knachel, ed., The Case of the Commonwealth of England, Stated, By Marchamont Nedham, Washington: The Folger Shakespeare Library, 1969, pp. xvif.

25. F.W.M. Draper, Four Centuries of Merchant Taylors' School 1561-1961, London: Oxford University Press, 1962, p. 58.

26. Draper, Merchant Taylors', p. 57.

27. Joseph Frank, Hobbled Pegasus, Albuquerque: The University of New Mexico Press, 1968, p. 117.

28. Wood, pp. 1180f. Firth, in DNB, says that "During the early part of his career Nedham also studied medicine." I at one time conjectured that between his stint at Merchant Taylors' and his clerkship at Gray's Inn

Nedham might have spent a few months at Leyden. My evidence, in addition to the fact that in 1645 he began to practice medicine, was that when he fled to Holland in 1660, he apparently had friends there; and that in the mid-1660's, when he got involved in medical polemics, he showed considerable knowledge of the chemical principles taught at Leyden. Nedham, however, was never noted for his modesty, and nowhere does he mention such prestigious training; nor do any of his contemporaries, including Wood, credit him with it. Also, in his Preface to Bolnest's *Medicina Instaurata* he mocks at those physicians who go abroad to get medical degrees, rather than learning by experience at home. Finally, Nedham gives every evidence of agreeing with Thomas Sydenham, England's most famous mid-seventeenth-century doctor, that "the physician who earnestly studies, with his own eyes-and not through the medium of books-the natural phenomena of the different diseases, must necessarily excel in the art of discovering what, in any given case, are the true indications as to the remedial measures that should be employed." (Quoted in Brian Inglis, *A History of Medicine*, London: Weidenfeld and Nicolson, 1965, p. 99.

29. *Mercurius Anti-Britanicus* and *Aulicus, his Hue and Cry Sent forth after Britanicus*. In 1652 Nedham was officially admitted to Gray's Inn as "of the city of Westminster, gent." (Firth, *DNB*).

30. *Aulicus, his Hue and Cry Sent forth after Britanicus*.

31. Wood, p. 1183.

32. Firth, *DNB*.

CHAPTER II

FIRST MOVEMENT-1643-1646

The first shot of the English Civil War was fired in August 1642. The next six months proved that the war would not be short. Charles I, despite his own mistakes in public relations, believed in the power of propaganda. In January 1643 he had his closest advisers arrange for the publication in Oxford of a weekly newspaper, Mercurius Aulicus. Its first editor was Dr. Peter Heylyn, formerly of Burford. Heylyn promptly hired John Berkenhead, an equally ardent Laudian and Royalist, who from Aulicus's start to its demise in 1645 did most of the writing. In fact, after a month Heylyn gave up all editorial responsibility. Turning out a weekly newspaper could be, and in most cases was, a one-man job, but Berkenhead received help from George Digby, one of Charles's Secretaries of State, and intermittenly from others high in the Royalist Court.[1] Consequently, during its first two years the news printed in Aulicus, no matter how slanted, had an aura of authenticity, often of true insiderness. Moreover, Berkenhead was a glib and spicy writer. Demand for the paper in London was high, and hundreds of copies were weekly smuggled into the city, where it normally sold for three times the penny charged for the London journals.[2] Throughout 1643 and 1644 it probably averaged 1,000 to 1,500 copies a week, with each copy having several readers.[3] Thus Mercurius Aulicus was a real thorn in Parliament's flesh, and Nedham was chosen to help sterilize, if not remove, it.

Berkenhead was skilled in mud-slinging and ridicule, in magnifying the King's victories and belittling those of Parliament, and in widening the rifts and exacerbating the jealousies within the loose anti-Royalist coalition--rifts and jealousies about which the Court's agents in London kept him well informed. By the summer of 1643 the leaders of that Parliamentary coalition felt sufficiently needled and threatened to set up their own newspaper. Since late 1641 a variety of weeklies published in London had provided English news, usually with a pro-Parliament bias. But now a journal of rebuttal rather than of news seemed necessary. By then as many as 500 copies of <u>Aulicus</u> were being weekly reprinted in London, in addition to those smuggled into the city, thus making its divisive thrusts even more omnious.[4]

In Parliament, at that pivotal moment, essentially three incipent parties or loose coalitions were functioning: a war party that was openly anti-Royalist and even displayed a few republican tendencies; a peace party that favored a quick accommodation with the King; and a middle group that held the balance of power, though it tilted to the left. This middle group was led by John Pym, a political operator whose tactics foreshadowed those of Lyndon Johnson when he was Majority Leader of the United States Senate in the 1950's.[5]

The Earl of Essex, the commanding general of the Parliamentary armies, had been Pym's selection, and both were coming under strident criticism from left and right. <u>Aulicus</u> exploited this by attacking Essex, and thereby Pym's leadership of Parliament. In April, Berkenhead claimed that both civilians and soldiers had lost confidence in the General, and that Pym could not even pick a capable field commander. <u>Aulicus</u> labelled Essex's victory at Reading that spring as pyrrhic, and claimed that he had to dig five large but secret pits in which "to cast the greatest part of those poore wretches...for feare the true numbers of the slaine might disconsolate their party."[6] Berkenhead also stepped up his campaign of guilt by association by linking Pym with the most flamboyant of the Republicans, Henry Marten, with Cromwell, a bloody boor who delighted in defacing churches, and with a variety of "atheists" and "radicals."

Probably at the suggestion of Pym, and almost certainly with the special blessing of Essex, <u>Mercurius Britanicus</u> was launched at the end of August 1643.[7] Berkenhead promptly pointed out that the second word was misspelled, with the result that <u>Britanicus</u> never did pick up its missing "n."[8] Unlike the other weeklies then published in London but like <u>Aulicus</u>, it was launched not by one man but by four or five "conspirators in wit."[9] One of them was Nedham; and his boss, at the start, was Captain Thomas Audley.

An unfriendly journalist described Audley as a "short, swarthy, chess-nut colour'd" man, and claimed that his military experience had been acquired mainly in London pubs, as he was not the sort to risk life or limb in battle.[10] In early 1639 Audley had lived in Bloomsbury, and soon found himself in some sort of trouble for spreading "libels and Scottish phamphlets."[11] Not only did Audley look like Nedham, but both had the ability to land on their feet. In the autumn of 1644, partly as insurance against any editorial mistakes, Audley became a deputy liscenser of the press under John Rushworth. Late in 1646 he briefly edited another weekly.[12] Thereafter I can find no record of him, though I assume he survived. Whatever Audley's fate, within a year of the founding of <u>Mercurius Britanicus</u> Nedham was in charge and doing most of the work*

From the start <u>Britanicus</u> was closer to <u>Aulicus</u> than to the London newspapers. Its main purpose was to counter Berkenhead, to negate the negative. Within a few months Audley and Nedham were devoting about six of their weekly pages to answering and smearing Berkenhead, only two to summarizing the news. Apparently this worked, for

---

* In discussing Nedham's role as a newspaper editor from 1643 to 1660, I rely very heavily on my own <u>The Beginnings of the English Newspaper, 1620-1660</u> (Harvard, 1961). In fact, some of my paraphrases from that book are so close that they constitute self-plagiarism.

<u>Britanicus</u> quickly became the best selling of the Parliamentary journals.[13]

    A major reason for this popularity was the unexpected style of <u>Britanicus,</u> since its language was often caustic, outspoken, varied. The first number indulged in heavily loaded case histories of certain Lords who had deserted to Oxford. The third featured an assualt on the Queen, and the tenth strongly criticized the King by stressing the very bad advice he was receiving. Such attacks were headier items than the more oblique and subdued comments in other London weeklies. Mainly, however, Audley and Nedham shot at Berkenhead directly by name-calling and indirectly by refuting his stories. When <u>Aulicus</u> called attention to the small number of <u>MP's</u>, <u>Britanicus</u> reacted by claiming that there were 18 in the House of Lords, 160 in the House of Commons, and that it was the Oxford Parliament that was a mockery of representative government. When <u>Aulicus</u> published a poignant letter from the wife of a soldier in the Parliamentary army, <u>Britanicus</u> printed a profane counterpart from a Cavalier's wife.[14]

    By the spring of 1644 some of the rifts in the Parliamentary coalition began to be reflected in <u>Britanicus</u>. Up to then, by concentrating on attacking Berkenhead and denigrating the Royalist cause and the King's evil advisers, Audley and Nedham had been able to postpone taking sides between the peace and war parties, Presbyterian and Independent, Parliament and army. But Pym died at the end of 1643, and the absence of his strong hand was soon evidenced by the disintegration of the middle group in Parliament. Nedham seemingly anticipated the consequent weakening of the anti-Royalist coalition, for the concluding lines of his elegy to Pym are unintentionally humorous in their praise of him as a public force rather than a private individual:

    Teares are too narrow drops for him,
    And private sighes too strait for Pym;
    None can completely Pym lament,
    But something like a Parliament,

> The publike sorrow of a State
> Is but a griefe commensurate,
> We must enacted passions have,
> And laws for weeping at his grave.[15]

For Aulicus Pym's death was a happy event: "loaded with various diseases," he made "a most loathsome and foule carkasse."[16] John Taylor reacted in a similar way. In Mercurius Aquaticus; Or, The Water-Poets Answer To All That Hath or shall be Writ by Mercuricus Britanicus, he reprinted this sixteenth number of Britanicus, prolixly refuted it item by item, and concluded with, "And so having cost my Reader halfe an hower, and my selfe an afternoone...I leave you as I found you, fit only to write verses on the Death of Mr. Pym."[17] Though Taylor did not mention Nedham by name, this was the first of many attacks, spread over thirty-five years, against him.

For three weeks at the beginning of 1644 Audley and Nedham did not publish their paper, partly because Aulicus had become erratic in its publication.[18] Nedham then announced his return:

> I tooke up my pen for disabusing his Majesty, and for disbishiping and dispoping his good subjects, and for taking off the vizards and vailes and disguises which the Scribes and Pharisees at Oxford had put upon a treasonable and popish cause, and I laid it down as freely; but I feel the generation is restless, alwaies plotting and printing; I see Aulicus will be...comming abroad still.[19]

So Nedham went back to refuting Aulicus. Now he emphasized his rival's vicissitudes: George Digby was supplanting Berkenhead, Berkenhead had been fired, Berkenhead was journalistically dead, and Nedham printed a vulgar obituary, complete with urinalysis. Thereafter Britanicus gave less space to attacking the Royalist press and cause, more to boosting Parliament. In June 1644 Nedham cockily proclaimed this shift:

I shall now at the expiration of Aulicus make it my task to give you the faithfullest and most politicke Relations of the times I can, and to the best advantage of the Cause; and since the victory sits upon my Pen, I hope my Paper will be hereafter more acceptable to the Kingdom, for I have by an excellent and powerfull Providence led the people through the labyrinths of the enemies Plots, through all their Jesuiticall windings and turnings, through the Episcopall and Prelaticall pretences; I have taken off the Calumnies from a Parliament, the scandalls from an Assembly, and I have wiped off the aspersions from every honourable Member and Agent in this Cause, from the House of Commons to the House of Lords, from thence to the City, from the City to the Armies, from the Armies to Scotland...I have brought the secrets and sins of the Court abroad, from her Majestie to Mistris Crofts her very maid of honour, and from his Majesty to his very Barbour....And if another rise up in the disguise of a Court Intelligencer....I shall never do him the honour hereafter to put him in the fore leafe of my booke, but behinde me, and there let him wait at the back door of my Intelligence.[20]

Nedham was somewhat premature. <u>Aulicus</u> was not yet dead, and <u>Britanicus</u> was beginning to be identified with the war party and the militant Independents. In fact, four months earlier Nedham had anticipated this move to the left by writing a pamphlet against William Prynne. Prynne was now, and would continue to be for the next two-and-a-half decades, the pugnacious, legalistic, and untiring voice of Erastianism, despite the fact that in 1637 he had had an ear chopped off for opposing Laud. His dispute with Nedham shows how tangled the politics of the mid 1640's were, and how, incidentally, a man with the talents of a press agent could benefit from just such tangles.

Nathaniel Fiennes was the son of Lord Say, the most militant Independent in the House of Lords. The son was highly thought of by Pym and his allies, and in 1643 he was made governor of Bristol. In July Fiennes surrendered the city to Prince Rupert, an action that was probably justified militarily but which gave a strong impression of being, if not cowardly, at least premature. In December 1643 Fiennes was tried by a military court and condemned to death, then promptly pardoned.[21] Meanwhile, shortly before his trial both he and the self-justification he had written were violently assailed by Prynne and his equally conservative friend Clement Walker. Then in February 1644 Prynne's A Checke to Britannicus attacked Nedham for advising and supporting Fiennes. Fiennes, though he was later to be a victim of Pride's Purge, was at this time identified with the war party: not only was he his father's son, but the court-martial which condemned him, and which was under the thumb of the army high command, had almost certainly arranged for his immediate pardon by Essex. Hence Prynne and Walker, alarmed at the revolutionary direction in which the civil war seemed to be heading, were using the Fiennes case to belabor the militants in Parliament and army.

It was into the imbroglio that Nedham did not stumble but stepped. Though he gave almost no space to Fiennes in Britanicus, he advised him before and during his trial, and in February came into the open with A Checke to the Checker of Britanicus. In this, his first pamphlet, he was taking a stand that the immediate future lay with the Independents and the leaders of the army. He was right.

Nedham was motivated by money as well as by political foresight. Prynne began his Checke with the charge that "Britannicus during his last weekes silence hath been visiting Nath: Fiennes," and that Fiennes "hath bribed Britannicus to trumpet forth his unknowne eminent deserts and publicke vertues to the people." Prynne went on the say that Nedham had accepted similar bribes to give "puffs" for other clients. A year later John Cleveland echoed Prynne when he accused Britanicus of currying favors by printing flattering write-ups of two army leaders.[22] A few other London journalists turned out to be equally buyable,[23] but Nedham was the first—and most successful—Interregnum press agent.

In a *Checke to the Checker* he earned his fee. The tone of this thirty-page pamphlet is moderate, often condescending, and ostensibly objective. "I shall write," Nedham announces, "not to contradict, provoke, contend with, or exasperate the pen of any." Unlike Prynne, he will uphold the "Equity and fairer side" of the law, not just its letter. He gives eight pro-Fiennes arguments, then cites and answers seven arguments against Essex's pardon. His concluding pages question the legal knowledge and motives of those attacking Fiennes. It is an effective performance: the author is restrained, he avoids both wit and rancor, and he displays his Gray's Inn training without flamboyance.

Nedham was versatile. In January 1645 he again attacked Prynne, this time obliquely. Prynne had just published a violent attack on the Independents: *Truth Triumphing over Falsehood, Antiquity over Novelty*. John Lilburne, rapidly becoming the loudest and most charismatic spokesman for the doctrine "salus populi suprema lex," immediately replied in *A Copie of a Letter...To Mr. William Prinne Esq*. In it, among other challenges, he announced that one of Prynne's friends "not long since told me that there was as great a disproportion betwixt you [Prynne] and me...as there is betwixt a tall Cedar and a little shrub...I replyed, goe you, and tell this tall Cedar the little shrub will have a bout with him." Th specific bout Lilburne proposed was a public debate on the question of religious toleration.[24] Ten days later M.N.—almost certainly Marchamont Nedham—spoke out in behalf of the little shrub.

In 1638 Lilburne had written a verbose fundamentalist attack on the "prelatical church" in which he supported separation of church and state.[25] Someone, probably Nedham, arranged for the reprinting of this *Answer to Nine Arguments*, and its short preface is signed by M.N. Here, in an extremely pious style, he announced that, "The Providence of God...[has] brought to my hand the ensuing matter." Thus he is now in a position properly to praise Lilburne as a true patriot and to attack "carnall possessours," as well as clergymen and lawyers.

The opposite of this pious style was Nedham's sustained voice in *Britanicus*, especially when he was sparring with Berkenhead. *Aulicus* survived until September 1645, leaving behind a bill for ₤90 which the printer tried to collect from Charles II after the Restoration.[26] Until then, however, Berkenhead continued to sow seeds of dissension. He now shed tears over the Earl of Essex, since he was about to be demoted by the newly organized high command of the army, and he regularly tried to exacerbate the grievances between Presbyterian and Independent, Parliament and army, England and Scotland. He also magnified a variety of personal feuds among the London "grandees," reserving some of his strongest epithets for Cromwell. Cromwell was a coward, bully, boor, and tyrant, and he and his "barbarous crew of Brownists" filled Lincoln Cathedral with "their own and horses dung."[27] Berkenhead was ready and able not only to use Independent dung but also rumors, loaded anecdotes, and atrocity stories. Predictably most atrocious was the militants' mounting disrespect for the King, including the growing possibility that they were contriving to murder him.

Yet one is aware of the cracks in Berkenhead's bold facade. Throughout its final year *Aulicus* contained little news from Oxford or of the over-all status of the Royalist cause. Indecisive skirmishes consistently became major Royalist victories. Further, the paper's London reprint appeared infrequently, and attempts to smuggle *Aulicus* into the metropolis were increasingly thwarted. Just before *Aulicus* expired, *Britanicus* claimed it was rare enough to cost sixpence a copy in London.28 During its final three months, when Oxford was under siege, it came out only three times. Apparently undaunted, Berkenhead retained his bravado, not only by what he had to say but by so numbering his pages that the run seemed to be gapless, thereby suggesting that the reader, not Aulicus, had skipped certain weeks.

Still, the story of Mericurius Britanicus remained closely interwoven with that of Aulicus. Late in 1644 one London weekly even reported that:

> ...[Charles] hath sent Secretary Nicholas...to Master Aulicus to require him to forbeare writing any more, till his Majesties pleasure be further knowne: the reason of this I cannot give you: It cannot sure to be to save the 30 pound per annum, the stipent His Majesty allowed him for writing his weekly pamphlet: It is done rather to silence Britanicus, who hath so plentifully laid open the vices at court, and who took the liberty to do so because Aulicus did so abuse Parliament....29

But a note of regret crept into Britanicus whenever Aulicus failed to appear, one of relief when it reappeared. Even when Nedham reached a crescendo of invective, one can sense a feeling of camaraderie between him and Berkenhead:

> But harke ye, thou mathematicall liar, that framest lies of all dimensions, long, broad and profound lies, and then playest the botcher, the quibling pricklouse every weeke in tacking and stitching them together; I tell thee (Berkenhead) thou art a knowne notorious odious forger: and though I will not say thou art (in thine own language) the sonne of an Egyptian whore, yet all the world knowes thou art an underling pimpe to the whore of Babylon, and thy conscience an arrant prostitute for base ends. This is truth, not railing.30

As part of this zestful competition Nedham could be as vicious and distorted as Berkenhead, and his defense of Laud's execution was a reverse image of Berkenhead's diatrabe against it. Nedham once parodied a speech by Charles, to which Berkenhead responded with predictable outrage.[31] The infighting between the two weeklies even involved the American colonies. In the summer of 1644 *Aulicus* twice commented that the people of New England were shocked by the language of *Britanicus*. As part of his evidence Berkenhead cited a published letter from a Massachusetts minister that placed some of the blame for God's wrath against England on Nedham and his colleagues.[32] Three times Nedham replied to this charge, putting most of the onus for God's alleged wrath on Berkenhead, and claiming that the whole affair was part of an Oxford plot to discredit *Britanicus* and the cause for which it spoke.[33]

That cause, that loose coalition, grew steadily more fragmented, then internecine, as the military power of the Royalists was crushed. At first Nedham did his best not to fall off his swaying political tightrope by showing himself more aware of Presbyterian sensibilities: he scattered a few kind words for the Solemn League and Covenant, praised certain generals (possibly for a fee) who were noted for their Presbyterian leanings, and even hinted that he would not oppose a Presbyterian settlement of the church.[34] Also on several occasions he criticized freedom of speech, and intermittently he questioned the principle of religious toleration by warning against the dangers implicit in sectarian preaching.[35]

But such conservative sops were the exception. Nedham quickly detected in which direction the political winds were blowing, and at the end of 1644 he became overtly pro-Independent. In the dispute between Cromwell and Manchester, Nedham supported the former, and he strongly advocated the new-modelling of the army.[36] But it was in his treatment of the King that Nedham most clearly revealed his current stance. As late as November he was still stressing the guilt of Charles's "evil advisers," but in January 1645 he shifted his attack so that it was directly-and repeatedly-aimed at the King himself. Charles, wrote Nedham, was a conspirator, possibly a traitor, and it would be well for England if his son took over the throne.[37] In June these accusations reached a temporary climax in Nedham's lengthy and detailed charge that the King was an active agent of International Catholicism.[38]

Nedham's attacks on Charles carried with them a series of radical opinions, among them that further negotiations between Parliament and King would now be futile, that the monopoly of the Merchant Adventurers was evil, and that "salus populi" was indeed the "suprema lex" of England.[39] He also informed his readers that he was not being told by Parliament or army what to write, that he was his own boss.[40] And he assured them that he had not been censored or censured for being too bold against the King.[41]

As Nedham became more prominent and as he moved toward the left, he became the target for Royalist barbs. <u>Aulicus</u> of course attacked him, as did a series of short-lived Royalist weeklies. Early in 1645 John Cleveland's <u>The Character of a London Diurnal</u> fulminated against the London press, and Nedham constituted part of the ugly and generalized "character" that emerges as a typical editor.[42] In February George Wither's <u>The Great Assises Holden in Parnassus by Apollo and His Assesors</u> was just as generalized. The poetry represents Wither at his verbose and pompous worst, as can be seen in this versified mixture of dislike for what Nedham writes and implied admiration for Nedham's wit:

   A Malefactour then receiv'd command,
   Before the Barre to elevate his hand;
   <u>Mercurius Britanicus</u> by name,
   Was hee, who first was call'd to play his
     game:
   Then <u>Edmund Spenser</u> Clarke of the Assise
   Read the Endictment loud, which did comprise
   Matters of scandall, and contempt extreme,

>Done against the Dignitie, and Diademe
>Of great Apollo, and that legall course,
>Which throughout all Parnasssus was in force.
>For use of Mercury hee was acus'd,
>Which weekely hee into his inke infus'd,
>Thereby to murther, and destroy the fame
>Of many, with strange obloquie, and shame.
>Hee likewise was accus'd, to have purloin'd
>Some drachmes of wit, with a felonious mind,
>From Helicon, which hee in Satyrs mixt,
>To make some laugh, and others deepely
>   vext.[43]

In May John Taylor again attacked Britanicus, this time in Rebels Anathematized and Anatomized. With his typical rollicking-and seeimingly endless-vehemence he berates Nedham:

>That poyson-framing Hownd Britannicus,
>That weekly snarling whelpe of Cerberus,
>That Microcosme of Morbus Gallicus,
>That Lernean venom'd Snake of Erebus.
>The Devill oft doth good, against his will,
>So you and he doth, for your damn'd despight
>Proves the King's good, although you wish him
>   ill,
>And makes his royall splendour shine more
>   bright.

Wood, looking back at this part of Nedham's career, says that, "Soon after siding with the rout and scum of the people, he made them weekly sport by railing at all that was noble, in...Merc. Britan. wherein his endeavours were to sacrifice the fame of some lord, or person of quality, nay of the King himself, to the beast of many heads."[44] In late 1645 and most of 1646 the number of direct attacks on Nedham increased. From a Royalist point of view he deserved them.

The King's defeat at the Battle of Naseby in June 1645 both sharpened and complicated the divisions within the Parliamentary coalition. Now that the principal enemy seemed defeated, the various anti-Royalist groups, as well as those who feared that events had already moved too far and too quickly away from England's traditional arrangements, were free to fight among themselves. Paradoxically, Charles held a stronger position and possessed more options than he had since 1640.

In July Nedham used <u>Britanicus</u> to quote extensively from, and bitingly to comment on, the King's private correspondence captured at Naseby.[45] Emboldened by the jubilant reactions to these letters among the Independents and militants and by the rout of the Royalist armies, Nedham early in August printed the following "wanted" notice:

> If any man can bring any tale or tiding of a wilfull King, which hath gone astray these foure years from his Parliament, with a guilty Conscience, bloody Hands, a Heart full of broken Vowes and Protestations: If these marks be not sufficient, there is another in the mouth: for bid him speak, and you will soon know him [Charles stuttered]: Then give notice to Britanicus, and you shall be well paid for your paines. So God save the Parliament.[46]

Nedham was not only blaspheming God's anointed, he was grinning as he did it. The repurcussions were prompt.

The House of Lords immediately objected, and Robert White, the printer of <u>Britanicus</u>, was sent to the Fleet Prison. White blamed <u>Audley</u>, who for a year had been acting as Rushworth's deputy, with the specific job of licensing <u>Britanicus</u>. Audley in turn put the blame on Nedham, who, he said, had neglected his suggestion that the offending passage be altered. Nedham, however, was let off with an official reprimand, while Audley was sentenced to a short stay in the Gatehouse.[47] Probably Audley, possibly Nedham, then wrote a short, standardized, and extremely humble <u>Apologie To all Well-affected people</u>. The author confessed, "I have overshot myself, though I hope, not beyond Recovery"--a confession which

Berkenhead labelled "the vomitting out of poysoned Crocodile teares."[48]

The strangest published product of this contretemps appeared two days after the *Apologie*: *Aulicus His Hue and Cry Sent forth after Britanicus*. This was the most effective attack on Nedham to date: it names him specifically, mocks the *Apologie*, and refutes his attack on the King. It was duly entered in the Stationer's Register and thus published with some sort of official approval. Almost certainly the author was John Berkenhead. The allegedly strict censorship arrangements of the 1640's were nicely blessed with carelessness, laxness, inconsistency. Not only had Berkenhead been sanctioned, but Audley, upon apologizing to the Lords, was released after only a week in the Gatehouse, on the condition that he not license any more newsbooks. The imprimatur of Gilbert Mabbott then appeared on *Britanicus*, but three months later Audley was again licensing Nedham's weekly.[49]

In August 1645, after skipping only one number, *Britanicus* was back on the streets of London, again attacking *Aulicus*, the Royalists, the King. Nedham even claimed that any criticism of *Britanicus* was a sign of "Malignancie."[50] In September his final full-fledged diatribe against *Aulicus* appeared, followed a week later by a mocking notice of his rival's demise; but it was an obituary that contained a note of regret.[51] Thereafter *Britanicus* temporarily resembled the other London weeklies, though Nedham devoted more space than they to news from Westminister. Even so, he was careful not to take too firm a stand, in late 1645, on the squabbles between Presbyterian and Independent. He did worry about the impending breach with the Scots, but in four consecutive numbers he skillfully explained why no foreign countries (and the Scots were not quite foreigners) were likely to aid the King's cause.[52] In going out of his way to praise Parliament, Nedham twice briefly questioned the right of the people to influence their rulers by petitions, and immediately several London papers came to the defence of their readers by assailing him.[53]

Then a new <u>Mecurius Aulicus</u>, not by Berkenhead, for three months enabled Nedham to fill many of his pages with counterattacks against a safely Royalist opponent. But he was again becoming openly convinced that the Independent wave of the future was about to crest, and he even came to the support of the now notorious John Lilburne.[54] Recurrently in the spring of 1646 he expressed the conviction that the defeat of the Royalists should be total: that any peace negotiations should be as militantly conducted as the later stages of the war had been.[55] In March he underlined this by warning the Independents to be wary of Royalist support and entrapment.[56] In April, in a lighter key, he referred to the Queen as "a Petty-coat Machiavel." In May, after Charles had fled to the Scots, Nedham wrote that he was not surprised and that revenge must be taken against the promoters of civil war: "that a strict account be required for the blood of all the Saints."[57] In what turned out to be the final issue of <u>Mercurius Britanicus</u>--Number 130, May 11-18, 1646--Nedham berated the King, using language and concepts that were still almost two years ahead of time. Nedham and Audley were brought before the House of Lords. Audley disclaimed any responsibility for this number of <u>Britanicus</u>, which had not been properly licenced, and he was immediately released. Nedham went to jail.[58]

The charge against him was publishing "divers passages between the two Houses of Parliament and other scandalous particulars not fit to be tolerated." But in this instance his real offense was political prematurity. He was arrested by order of the House of Lords, he confessed to the authorship of the last eighty numbers of <u>Mercurius Britanicus</u>, and on May 23 he was committed to Fleet Prison.[59] From there he promptly wrote Lord Denbigh, asking him to present to the House of Lords a petition "declaring that whatever errors may have fallen from his [Nedham's] pen, neither the desires of his friends nor the temptations of others could ever make him swerve from his loyalty to that right honourable house."[60] On June 4 he was released, on condition "that he shall not write any more Pamphlets without Leave of this House [of Lords] first obtained."[61] This ban included the editing of a weekly newspaper, and Nedham was ordered to post a bond of ₺200 for his good behavior.[62]

This was not a severe punishment, and Nedham was obedient. He had begun to practice medicine part time in 1645; now he took it up full time.[63] Then in 1647 he returned to journalism, this time on the side of the King. In retrospect, the Independents should have seen that he served a much longer sentence in jail or was rewarded instead of punished.

Nedham had been responsible for the last eighty numbers of <u>Mercurius Britanicus</u>, and probably for most of the preceding fifty he had written the news which Audley gathered in Westminster.[64] During these three years Nedham did much to modernize the English newspaper. He and Berkenhead set an example for more vigorous and colorful writing, as they did for such nineteenth- and twentieth-century journalistic practices as carefully planted rumors, trial balloons, supposedly authentic gossip, destructive innuendos, and blatently political atrocity stories. Nedham, by being conspicuous, also diverted a certain amount of official attention and heat to himself, thus allowing the more cautious London weeklies a little more leeway. One of his Royalist opponents charged that Nedham was paid ₺3 a week to edit <u>Britanicus</u>,[65] five times the amount the King was giving Berkenhead. Cumulatively his services to the militants in Parliament and army were worth this large sum.

Nedham's effectiveness is underlined by the number and violence of the attacks against him during his final year as editor of <u>Britanicus</u>. The many fly-by-night Royalist weeklies were especially vehement. In the summer of 1645, for instance, Mercurius Anti-Britanicus lived up to its title for the three numbers it survived.[66] Nedham's vicissitudes in May 1646 drew much gloating comment. In July Francis Wortley's Characters and Elegies called Nedham a Jew, referred to his "sullen and dogged wit," and recommended that "his hands and feet be as sacrifices cut off, and hung up, to pay for the Treasons of his pen and tongue."[67] Early in 1647 Wortley, still angry, published Mercurius Britanicus His Welcome to Hell: With the Devills Blessing to Britanicus. Wortley's poetry here excels that of Wither and Taylor:

> Thus shalt thou no good entertainment lack,
> And brave Guy faux with famous Ravillack
> Shall wait on thee from board unto thy bed,
> And each of them shall be thy Ganimed.

And from Nedham's "Epitaph":

> Here lies Britanicus, Hell's barking cur,
> That son of Beliall, who kept damned stir;
> And every Monday spent his stock of spleen,
> In venomous railing on the King and Queen.
> Who, though they both in goodness may forgive him,
> Yet (for his safety) wee'l [Hell] receive him.[68]

Wortley was prophetic: in September 1647 the King forgave Nedham.

Footnotes   Chapter II

1. My material on Berkenhead and *Aulicus* comes from the excellent biography by P.W. Thomas: *Sir John Berkenhead 1617-1679: A Royalist Career in Politics and Polemics*, Oxford: At the Clarendon Press, 1969; supplemented by Frank, *BN*. A collection of *Mercurius Aulicus* has been compiled by Frederick J. Varley, Oxford: Basil Blackwell, 1948.

2. Thomas, *Berkenhead*, pp. 52ff.

3. Thomas, *Berkenhead*, p. 52, estimates that on some weeks the number of copies published could have reached 5,000. I think that is far too high, especially in view of the physical problems of printing and distribution. My own guess is that no run exceeded 3,000--and that figure is probably high.

4. Thomas, *Berkenhead*, p. 49. Milton commented on *Aulicus's* wide London circulation in his *Areopagitica* in November 1644 (*Complete Prose Works of John Milton*, New Haven: Yale University Press, 1959, II, 528). See also *Mercurius Britanicus*, #4, Sept. 12-19, 1643.

5. J.H. Hexter, *The Reign of King Pym*, Cambridge: Harvard University Press, 1941, is a fascinating account of Pym's leadership of the Long Parliament during its first three years. In one of his few references to Nedham, Hexter calls him a well-known liar.

6. Frank, *BN*, pp. 47f.

7. Frank, *BN*, p. 311; William M. Clyde, *The Struggle for Freedom of the Press From Caxton to Cromwell*, reprinted New York: Burt Franklin; 1970, p. 88.

8. Frank, *BN*, p. 49.

9. Frank, BN, pp. 311f.

10. Mercurius Anti-Britanicus, #3, ca. Aug. 18, 1645.

11. Clyde, Freedom of the Press, p. 45.

12. Frank, BN, p. 312. During 1644 Audley also contributed occasional pieces to another London journal, The Kingdomes Weekly Intelligencer.

13. This is implied by Wood and strongly corroborated by my own research into the newspapers of the mid-1640's.

14. Frank, BN, p. 50.

15. Mercurius Britanicus, no. 16, Dec. 7-14, 1643.

16. Frank, BN, p. 51.

17. Reprinted in Works of John Taylor, the Water Poet, not included in the Folio Volume of 1630, Manchester: The Spenser Society, 1870-1878, Vol. V. Nedham replied to Taylor in Mercurius Britanicus, no. 21, Jan. 29-Feb. 5, 1644.

18. For the publication history of Aulicus, see Thomas, Berkenhead, pp. 238-244.

19. Brit., no. 21, Jan. 20-Feb. 4, 1644.

20. Brit., no. 39, June 10-17, 1644.

21. Frank, BN, p. 60f. Vernon F. Snow, Essex the Rebel, Lincoln: University of Nebraska Press, 1970, pp. 404-6.

22. John Cleveland, The Character of a London Diurnal, London, 1645.

23. Thomas, Berkenhead, p. 47. Lucy Hutchinson, Memoirs of the Life of Colonel Hutchinson, London: J.M. Dent & Sons, pp. 101f.

24. Joseph Frank, The Levellers, Cambridge: Harvard University Press, 1955, p. 46.

25. Frank, Levellers, pp. 21f.

26. Varley, Aulicus, p. ix.

27. Mercurius Aulicus, no. 38, Sept. 14-21, 1644.

28. Brit., no. 95, Aug. 25-Sept. 1, 1645. The True Character of Mercurius Aulicus, 1645, claimed that at the end a copy of Aulicus sold for as much as 18 pence in London.

29. The Kingdomes Weekly Intelligencer, no. 83, Nov. 26-Dec. 3, 1644. Other London papers spread the same rumor, one even adding that the King intended to put an end to Aulicus because of its "Notorious lies" [Frank, BN, p. 319].

30. Brit., no. 69, Feb. 3-10, 1645.

31. Brit., no. 35, May 6-13, 1644.

32. Mercurius Aulicus, no. 20, July 7-14, 1644; no. 32, July 28-Aug. 4, 1644. The letter in question was written by Nathaniel Rogers: A Letter discovering the cause of Gods continuing wrath against the Nation, dated Dec. 17, 1643, and published in London in the summer of 1644. Rogers inserts into his indignant and pious defense of Presbyterianism the following attack on Nedham.
>...I present to your wisest consideration the unhallowed passages that come forth in Mercurius Britanicus, of scornfull dishonour put upon the Name and Person of Him, who is by you acknowledged the Lords annointed...but to put bitter and most contemptuous scoffes upon His Royall

Person, is that which Davids heart could not beare...It's against not only the course of Scripture, but one article of the late Covenant.

33. *Brit.*, no. 46, July 29-Aug. 5, 1644; no. 47, Aug. 12-19, 1644; no. 49, Aug. 26-Sept. 2, 1644.

34. For instance, *Brit.*, no. 48, Aug. 19-26, 1644; no. 51, Sept. 23-30, 1644; no. 55, Oct. 21-28, 1644; no. 68, Jan. 27-Feb. 3, 1645; no. 72, Feb. 24-Mar. 3, 1645; no. 80, Apr. 21-28, 1645.

35. For instance, *Brit.*, no. 54, Oct. 14-21, 1644; no. 59, Nov. 18-25; 1644; no. 85, May 26-June 2, 1645; no. 86, June 9-16, 1645.

36. *Brit.*, no. 60, Dec. 2-9, 1644; no. 61, Dec. 9-16, 1644; no. 63, Dec. 13-20, 1644; no. 65, Jan. 6-13, 1645.

37. For instance, *Brit.*, no. 64, Dec. 30, 1644 - Jan. 6, 1645; no. 72, Feb. 24-March 3, 1645; no. 75, March 10-17, 1645; no. 79, Apr. 14-21, 1645.

38. *Brit.*, no. 88, June 23-30, 1645.

39. *Brit.*, no. 72, Feb. 24-March 3, 1645; no. 84, May 19-26, 1645; no. 74, March 10-17, 1645.

40. *Brit.*, no. 85, May 25-June 2, 1645.

41. *Brit.*, no. 86, June 9-16, 1645.

42. Several London editors answered Cleveland; Nedham was not one of them.

43. *The Great Assizes* has been reprinted at Oxford for the Luttrell Society by Basil Blackwell, 1948.

44. Wood, p. 1181.

45. See especially Brit., no. 91, July 21-28, 1645.

46. Brit., no. 92, July 28-Aug. 4, 1645.

47. Frank, BN, p. 99.

48. Mercurius Britanicus, His Apologie to all Well-affected People, licensed on Aug. 9, dated by Thomson, Aug. 11, and printed by Robert White - now out of jail. The short-lived weekly Mercurius Anti-Britanicus attributes the Apoligie to Audley. I cannot tell whether this conventional item was written by him or Nedham, though I strongly suspect that Audley was the author. It is also possible that Nedham spent a few days in jail (Firth, DNB).

49. Frank, BN, p. 99. For further details, see Clyde, Freedom of the Press, pp. 88ff.

50. Brit., no. 93, Aug. 11-18, 1645.

51. Brit., nos. 98 and 99, Sept. 15-29, 1645. After no. 100 there was a gap of a week, possibly because Nedham missed his Oxford punching bag.

52. Brit., no. 101, Oct. 13-20, 1645; nos. 104-107, Nov. 3-Dec. 1, 1645.

53. Brit., no. 106, Nov. 17-24, 1645; no. 107, Nov. 24-Dec. 1, 1645. Nedham replied to these attacks in no. 112, Dec. 29, 1645-Jan. 5, 1646.

54. Brit., no. 116, Jan. 26-Feb. 2, 1646.

55. Brit., no. 127, Apr. 20-27, 1646.

56. Brit., no. 120, Feb. 23-March 2, 1646. After this number there is a gap of a week, possibly the result of this item's tactlessness.

57. Brit., no. 129, May 4-11, 1646. The reference to the Queen is from no. 127, Apr. 20-27, 1646.

58. Frank, BN, p. 100.

59. Firth, DNB; Journal of the House of Lords, VIII, 321, 325.

60. Historical Manuscripts Commission, Fourth Report, p. 273.

61. Journal of the House of Lords, VIII, 355.

62. Firth, DNB.

63. Wood, p. 1181.

64. Clyde, Freedom of the Press, p. 90.

65. Mercurius Academicus, no. 6, Jan. 19-26, 1646.

66. The editor of Mercurius Anti-Britanicus was especially indignant about Nedham's irreverent treatment of the King's correspondence captured at Naseby, and refers to him as "once a week sacrificing to the beast of many heads the fame of some lord or person of quality, nay even of the King himself." (Quoted in Firth, DNB). Wood liked this passage enough to incorporate it verbatim in his biography of Nedham.

67. Francis Wortley, Characters and Elegies, London, 1646, pp. 26f.

68. This may partly duplicate an earlier work by Wortley, one which I have not seen: Britanicus his Blessing. Britanicus his

Welcome, published in Cambridge in Jan. 1646. Wood, p. 1184, dates 'Merc. Britanicus his Welcome to Hell' in late 1645. Two broadside poems from early 1647 also belatedly attack Nedham, but more good naturedly than Wortley: *The Poore Committee-Mans accompt* and *The Committee-Mans Complaint and the Scots Honest Usage*. The first has the "chorus":

> That this is true you need not doubt,
>   examine Mr. Needham;
> He'd tell you true, and sweare it too,
>   tis for the kingdomes freedome.

The second has a similar "chorus," and includes the stanza:

> This Needham is Britanicus,
>   so they mis-name the creature;
> There's scarce a car-man in the towne,
>   but dares proclaim him traytor.

(See Frank, *Hobbled Pegasus*, p. 165.)

Firth in *DNB* mentions another attack on Nedham, which may date from early 1647: 'On Britannicus his leap three Story high, and his escape from London.' This short poem appears in *The Works of Mr. John Cleveland*, London, 1687, p. 247. Though probably not by Cleveland, it is clever and relatively good natured -- as the opening lines can indicate:

> *Paul* from *Damascus* in a Basket slides,
> Cran'd by the Faithful Brethren down the sides
> Of their embattell'd Walls. *Britannicus*
> As loath to trust the *Brethren God with us*,
> Slides too, but yet more desp'rate, and yet thrives
> In his descent; needs must! The Devil drives.

CHAPTER III

SECOND MOVEMENT—1646-1649

Anthony á Wood sums up Nedham's final months as a newspaper editor with the mixed compliment that he had "become a popular man among the rout," and--shades of Captain Audley--that "he was commonly called Captain Nedham of Greys Inn, and what he said or wrote was looked upon as gospel." Wood goes on: "About that time he studied physic, followed the chymical way, and...began to practise it, and by that and his writing, maintained himself in a very genteel fashion."[1] Between June 1646 and September 1647 Nedham stayed out of journalism--and out of trouble. Apparently he prospered as a doctor, though the controversial medical tract he wrote in 1665 is much stronger in theory than in clinical details.

He also wrote three pamphlets. The first was published in July 1646. Signed "By M.N. Med.Pr.," it was printed by his former colleague Robert White, and presumably approved by the House of Lords. Independencie No Schimse is a vigorous plea for religious toleration, in the form of a reply to John Vicars' The Schismatick Sifted and, indirectly, to Thomas Edwards Gangraena. Vicars and Edwards were reactionary Presbyterians who viewed with wild alarm and in great detail the growth of heretical sects in London. Edwards, in fact, following what Vicars called the "practical way" of writing, collected and described nearly three-hundred "dangerous" opinions circulating in London.

Nedham addresses his tract to Vicars, beginning abruptly with "You mean well, but you write ill." then for a dozen pages he demolishes Vicars' main arguments, generally using vehemence rather than vituperation to state his case against bigotry. For instance:

> I observe there is a great noise made of Schisme here among us: Thus the Papists charged the Protestants with schisme upon Luthers Reformation, and a long time after, till the slander became as threadbare, as the proofs of it were weak. Just so now deal the Presbyterians with their brethren, whom they nickname Independents: and whosoever traces Ecclesiastical history, shall find it hath ever been Satans policie, upon any irradiations of Divine light, immediately to brand it for schisme; which is the main reason why Reformation hath been so often near the birth, and yet not strength to bring it forth. I am perswaded, though we should hear a voice from heaven as John did, saying, Come out of her my people, yet the Devil would beg leave to be a lying spirit in the mouths of some, to brand them for schismaticks.

In sentences suggestive of the diction and ideas of William Walwyn, the most skeptical and intellectual of the Leveller leaders, Nedham asks:

> How dare you call it a Deceitful trick of impudent Imposters to look after more light? We should all be Seekers in this kinde: Had former years muzled themselves in a contentation in that light they then had, where then had been this light we now enjoy toward a Reformation?

And he answers:

> Take heed therefore lest while ye raile against new lights ye work despight to the Spirit of God. To Quench it in a mans self is a great sin, but to labour to quench it in others, to blaspheme, and cause it to be blasphemed by others, is that sin which (our Savour sayes) shall never be forgiven.

Over-all, Nedham's plea for religious toleration is almost Miltonic, including such tart asides as "Mr. Edwards indeed has been raking in the Kennel, but hath fouled himself most." In passing, Nedham briefly praises Milton's friend, John Goodwin, an outspoken minister with whom Nedham was to tangle ten years later. Now, however, he strongly supports him and other Independents by name, though in his capacity as a spy for Cromwell in the mid-1650's Nedham would help to put one of them, Sidrach Simpson, behind bars.[2]

Thus in July 1646 Dr. Nedham was unequivocally tolerationist and anti-Presbyterian. During the ensuing ten months he began to reconsider his position. The result was his next pamphlet, the equivocal <u>The Case of the Kingdom Stated, According to the Proper Interest of the severall Parties Ingaged</u>. Nedham wrote it in May; it appeared in June, with no author's or printer's name on the title-page, and almost certainly without the sanction of the House of Lords. The sub-title announces, in typical Nedham fashion, that this will be "A peece of Rare Observation and Contexture, wherein all men are equally Concerned." The eighteen closely reasoned and clearly written pages almost justify this boast. Nedham employs logic, law, history, plus a wide variety of rhetorical devices, to state his expedient argument and to try to realign the forces then battling for control of England.

<u>The Case of the Kingdom</u> is divided into four parts, the first of which is 'The Interest of the King and his Party.' Nedham urges the Royalists to ditch the Presbyterians and to join the Independents. The former are fundamentally against the monarchy and a "proper" civil government. The latter, in contrast, will not let the church dominate the state, and they will permit liberty of conscience, including certain rights for the Episcopal church and its bishops. Moreover, the Independents do not hate the monarchy, and their alliance with the King might dampen the "fury" of the Presbyterians. Therefore, "since the king hath no hope of remedy from his Friends here at home, or abroad, his true Interest at present is, by some

means or other, to close with that [the Independent] Party."

Part II, 'The Interest of the Presbyter and his Party,' energetically assails the "compulsive power" in religion. Since all men are fallible, persecution is unjust, the concept of religious conformity is sterile and stupid, and oppression "makes men mad... Therefore where we see any weaker in Judgement than our Selves, we ought to look upon them as deplorable, not damnable." If the Presbyterians continue to fight against liberty of conscience and for their rigid form of established religion, and if they continue to "fulminate" against others "as Heretiques and Schismatiques, &c.," then they will "shipwreck in the Haven." Instead, the Presbyterians should cease to oppose the Independents; otherwise they will be beaten by them.

In Part III, 'The Interest of the Independent Party,' Nedham praises the Independents' belief in toleration and in the separation of church and state. Next, he urges them to combine with the Royalists in an anti-Presbyterian alliance. Bishops, he argues, are far less oppressive then presbyters, and insofar as the King will promise freedom of conscience, so will the enmity between him and the Independents diminish. "That which will Crown Independent interest (and which is indeed true Parliamentary Interest, though Presbyterians have another way) is, to reconcile the King upon such honourable Termes, that...he and they are in all reason obliged to down...the Dagon of a rigid Presbyterie."

The final part, 'The Interest of the City of London,' displays Nedham at his polemical best. He again opens with flattery. London "beares the name of the Metropolis of England, the Royall Chamber, the grand Emporium, the universall Exchange for Traffick," and "her sole interest" is a free and flourishing trade. Consequently its businessmen should not tie themselves too closely to any single faction. Nor should they remain politically different from the rest of England--where the Presbyterians were less powerful. "The true Interest of the city is to coole by degrees toward a Presbyterie (not all at once, lest it be accounted Levity) and in the meane time to stand neutrall, ...to leave the Presbyterian cause to stand or fall, by Reason and open debate in Parliament." The result of such debate, if unimpeded by pressure from them and from the "mob," will be that "they may enjoy their City and Possessions without Envy, and the shaken Kingdom (they heeding still) may have time to settle, and recover the pristine wealth and splendour of a glorious Monarchie." Presumably the conservative Presbyterians who dominated the London economy could find this argument, with its fusion of nostalgia and promise of future profits, hard to resist. Nedham made it more enticing by reiterating that if the London economic establishment stayed out of politics for the time being, the country would soon be tranquil and prosperous.

At the end of The Case of the Kingdom Nedham cites Machiavelli, whose works he had been studying. By appealing to the potentially healing concept of religious toleration, a concept sacred to the Independents and the leaders of the army, and by basing his argument on the self-interest of the contending parties, Nedham was promoting a marriage of convenience between Royalists and Independents. But it was to be a marriage in which the Independents would be the junior partner. The former editor of Britanicus had come a long journey in ten months: The Case won prompt favor in the Royalist camp, and two more editions came out during the summer of 1647.[3] The most effective reply to it was aptly entitled Anti-Machiavelli, or Honesty against Policy.[4]

Early in June, after The Case was written but before it was published, Cornet Joyce captured the King in behalf of the army and of the Independents in Parliament. The events of the summer and autumn of 1647 were tumultuous and tangled: riots in London, anger and agitation in the army,

Presbyterian miscalculations in Parliament, the rise of the Leveller movement, along with an accelerated spin-off of revolutionary ideas shouted at street corners, whispered in caucuses, circulated in newspapers and pamphlets.[5] Charles did his best to play off one group against another, but his best was not very good. By combining myopia and arrogance in a conspicuous manner he made the Second Civil War and his own beheading first possible, then likely, then inevitable. Nedham chose this time to enlist in the Royalist cause.

But he had not yet fully signed on. Early in July he published <u>The Lawyer of Lincolnes-Inn Reformed: Or, An Apology for the Army</u>...William Prynne, the lawyer in need of reformation, had just written <u>IX Queries</u>, a violent attack on the army and a violent defense of eleven leaders of the Presbyterian party whom the army wanted to purge from Parliament. (Their saga is also complex and dramatic. After much maneuvering and counter-maneuvering they were expelled; Pride's Purge at the end of 1648 then completed the subjugation of Parliament to Cromwell and his military associates.)

Nedham begins his rebuttal of Prynne with high praise of the army. He then lengthily answers each of the nine queries, in the process derogating Prynne, the eleven MPs, and their Scottish and English supporters. Only indirectly does he support Charles and hint at his own shift: Joyce's delivery of the King to the army was the proper thing to do; otherwise he would be the prisoner of the unyielding Presbyterians. Thus, Nedham concludes, the army and its Independent allies are preserving both Parliament and Monarchy:

> so that if Cornet Joyce hath outwitted them [Parliament], though in a somewhat irregular way against the Letter of the Law, yet I trust this Nation will beare him out against all rigorous Lawyers, because of the happy consequence and effect it will produce both to

Prince and People, by setting a period to our tumultuous War, and hindring the progress of a second, which must necessarily involve us in inevitable ruine.

Needless to say, the Lawyer of Lincoln's Inn was not reformed by Nedham's expedient and contorted argument.

Was Nedham himself convinced? According to Wood, early in September 1647, just after his twenty-seventy birthday, "obtaining the favour of a known royalist to introduce him into his majesty's presence at Hampton Court...he then and there knelt before him, and desired forgiveness for what he had written against him and his cause: which being readily granted, he kiss'd his majesty's hand."[6] Charles was not just turning his other cheek or being saintly. Rather, he was hiring Nedham to edit a Royalist weekly, and the first number of Mercurius Pragmaticus appeared on September 21. Wood continues his account: it was "very witty, satyrical against the Presbyterians, and full of loyalty," and it "made him [Nedham] known to, and admired by the bravadoes and wits of those times."[7]

The former editor of Britanicus had certainly signaled this shift in his two most recent pamphlets. But why at this particularly dangerous moment? One reason is obvious: Nedham liked excitement and power. Being a doctor and occasional pamphleteer, after the headiness of editing Parliament's leading weekly, must have been anticlimactic. A second motive may have been money: Nedham also liked money, lots of it, and it is highly probable that Royalist sympathizers in London paid him well to shift to their cause.

A third motive may have been political: Nedham might really have felt that an Independent-Royalist alliance against the Presbyterians was feasible. But the King, at the time when Nedham knelt before him, was continuing negotiations with the Scots for an invasion of England,

45

while Cromwell was attracting the anger of the militants and radicals in Parliament and army for still dealing with Charles. Nedham's political logic may have made sense, but his timing was terrible. By late October Cromwell was convinced that trying to work with Charles was suicidal for both himself and his cause. The King's trial and execution were now only slightly more than a year away.*

In *The Case of the Kingdom* Nedham had suggested that if Charles would just "sit still...and blow the fire," he could ally himself with whatever group gave "most hope of indulgence to his prerogative and greatest possibility of favor to his friends." Charles was not sitting still, and Nedham was blowing the fire and fanning the flames. By this time censorship of the press, though still on the statute books, had broken down almost completely. A variety of Royalist weeklies briefly flourished, reaching a high point of seventeen separate newspapers in May and June of 1648.[8] Berkenhead returned to the journalistic wars as editor of the pugnacious *Mercurius Bellicus*; and *Mercurius Aulicus*, edited by Samuel Sheppard, a preacher turned poet turned journalist, staged a brief revival.[9] Nedham was about to join forces with several journalists whom he had castigated in *Britanicus* and who had responded in kind. One of them, the poet John Cleveland, helped Nedham on *Pragmaticus*, though he was sufficiently well known to spend much of his time in hiding.[10] (Nedham, too, was well known, and within a month the government managed to locate and jail his printer.)[11] Samuel Sheppard aided in the launching of the new weekly and regularly lent Nedham a hand.[12] This time his "conspirators in wit" were Royalists and literati.

---

* In my concluding chapter I try to examine the over-all pattern of Nedham's political logic and the problem of his bad timing. In certain ways he repeated, a decade later, his actions of the late 1640's.

Because the skein of Mercurius Pragmaticus's is tangled, I will merely suggest some of its bibliographical snarls. During a few intermittent weeks there were two papers with this name, sporadically reinforced by Mercurius Pragmaticus (For King Charles II, Mercurius Pragmaticus (For King Charls) (Charles without an "e"), Mercurius Pragmaticus For King Charls II (no "e" and no parentheses); then by the reappearance in the early 1650's of Mercurius Pragmaticus, and by the appearance, for one number, of Mercurius Pragmaticus Revived.[13] Writers moved from one weekly to another, publication was in most cases intermittent and, as the King's trial and execution approached, the censorship grew stricter, the problems of dodging the agents sent out to stifle the Royalist press adding to the confusion. But printing presses were small and portable, money always seemed available for expenses and bribes, and the editors had associates willing to hide them in the crowded rabbit warren of seventeenth-century London. The situation of the Royalist weeklies was similar to that of the underground press in Paris during the Nazi occupation, though the "Beagles of State" whom the army leaders unleashed to nose out their enemies were far more civilized and far less efficient than their German and Vichyite descendants.

The leading Royalist weeklies of 1647-48, Mercurius Melancholicus, Mercurius Elencticus, and Mercurius Pragmaticus, were vindictive, strident, unrestrained, and often indistinguishable. Yet Nedham's weekly was the most effective: its punches were more varied and harder-hitting, its fouls a little more damaging. From September 1647 to January 1649 Nedham was in charge of Pragmaticus. He did have the sporadic aid of Cleveland, Sheppard, and other Royalists wits but, more important, he had connections in Westminister--perhaps from his Britanicus days--who supplied him with information from the floor of the House of Commons and with gossip from cloakroom and caucus.[14] Nedham skillfully utilized this information and gossip. Pragmaticus described, sometimes gleefully, sometimes alarmedly, how the Independents exerted private pressures to get an impressively large attendance at certain sessions of the House of Commons; how they used intimidation, blackmail, and filibustering to win a Parliamentary majority; and how Cromwell and his cronies employed various devices, from sermons to troop movements, to influence public opinion. Nedham's scathing vignettes of the anti-Royalist leaders are equally skillful, and his account of an Independent caucus suddenly convened at 6:00 a.m. is still dramatic.[15]

Since the time Nedham knelt at the foot of the King he had been a full-fledged Royalist, but he never expressed any genuine liking for the Presbyterians, and the few times he praised their Scottish allies it was usually muted and qualified and, between the lines, condescending. He was slightly less antagonistic toward the Levellers, but only when they were attacking the Cromwellian "Grandees." "Is not this brave sport when rebels impeach each other?"; or, "Be not baffled bold Levellers, be constant and prosecute your claims ...against the perjured traitor Fairfax."[16] But *Pragmaticus* was consistently hostile to their democratic aspirations and programs, and one early number succinctly sets forth Nedham's current conservative view of recent English history.

> A Scot and Jesuite, joyn'd in hand,
>   First taught the world to say,
> That Subjects ought to have Command,
>   And Princes to Obey.
>
> These both agreed to have no King,
>   The Scotch-man he cries further,
> No Bishop; 'Tis a godly thing
>   States to reforme by Murther.
>
> Then th' Independent, meeke and slie,
>   Most lowly lies at Lurch,
> And so to put poore Jockie by
>   Resolves to have No Church.

> The King Dethron'd! The Subjects bleed!
>   The Church hath no aboad;
> Let me conclude, They're all agreed,
>   That sure there is No God.[17]

Nedham embellished each of the title-pages of the sixty-four numbers of <u>Mercurius Pragmaticus</u> which he wrote with four four-line-stanza poems on what can loosely be called current events. Their cumulative doggerel provides a fascinating close-up of the weekly shifts in political pressures during late 1647 and all of 1648. In 1661, when Nedham was trying to get back in the good graces of the Royalists, he republished them as a single long poem, entitled <u>A Short History of the English Revolution</u>. They also constitute a short history of Nedham's career as a Royalist editor.

The former editor of <u>Britanicus</u> and defender of Lilburne seemed to take special delight in pointing out--and pointing up--Cromwell's troubles with the Levellers and their agents in the army, the "Agitators." As early as October 1647 he wrote:

> And thus his [Cromwell's] dear Democraticks being left all in the suds, his face is now more toward an Aristocracie than Zion, which hath raised a deadly feud betwixt him and the Adjutators, who looke upon him as fallen from grace; especially since he hath used all his wit and power in the Army to suppresse them, now that he has served his ends upon them.[18]

In the same month Nedham accurately predicted Pride's Purge and Cromwell's subsequent troubles with Parliament:

> But Mr. Cromwell hath them [Parliament] in the Mill, grind they must, seeing that they are at his Beck who holds a Whip and a Bell over their guilty Heads....so that when he hath used them long enough under the name of Parliament, then (perhaps) they shall be

disbanded severall waies, that the Sword-men may stand for ever.[19]

In the spring of 1648 Nedham was equally prophetic, not only about the imminent Second Civil War but implicitly about the events of the early 1650's. At the same time, his dislike of the Presbyterians and the Scots continued to show through his Royalist rhetoric. For example:

> Yet I believe that Scots will be right honest...touching the person of the King; but I feare they may put a Slur upon us in this after-Game, in laboring to foist in their Presbytery, with its Appurtenances....Then let the English looke to themselves...for if it bee to bee brought in upon his Majestie's shoulders, upon pretence of restoring him, I suppose his Crowne and dignity is but in little more danger now he remaines in Carisbrooke Castle [as a captive of the English army] than if his person were in Edinburgh....[20]

Mercurius Pragmaticus was, from a Royalist point of view, off to a good start. It and its fellows exchanged mutual compliments, while the pro-Parliament weeklies countered with insults. Both compliments and insults were, however, almost always impersonal: "Pragmaticus" or "Melancholicus" rather than, say, Nedham or Cleveland. After three months as editor Nedham, under the name of "Pragmaticus," may have been the author of a closet-drama, The Levellers levell'd. Or, The Independent Conspiracie to root out Monarchie, published in December 1647. Wood attributes this hackneyed allegory to him, and it is something Nedham could have scribbled quickly and easily.*

---

* Because of Nedham's shifting politics and varied styles, it is very difficult to attribute a given work to him on the basis of either what it says or how it says it. In a few instances I have stated, with what seems to me adequate evidence, that a tract was not by him.

Lilburne--"John of London"--is the villainous leader of a plot to murder the King, aided by his pals Regicide and Patricide, not to mention Conspiracie, Treacherie, Democracie, and Impietie. The poetry in this largely verse "Interlude" is equally shallow and predictable:

> Bring forth the King, chop off his Head,
>   We ne're our wish shall gaine,
> Till we upon his trunk do tread,
>   His Blood must wash our Staine.

At the end even Fairfax turns against the Levellers, and Regicide laments that "The Heavens conspire against us, which way can we looke, and not behold our ruine?" The Levellers are levell'd, as they should be in a drama with the signature "Your Majesties most humble and dutifull Subject."[21]

Early in 1648 it was probably Nedham who wrote <u>Loyalty speakes Truth: Or, a Conference of the Grand Mercuries, Pragmaticus, Melancholicus, and Elen[c]ticus</u>. The tone and timing are appropriate to Nedham, and "Pragmaticus" is listed first in the sub-title. With much zest and a smattering of scurrility this eight-page "conference" bemoans the chaos and strife rending England, and blames the army, the Independents, and the radicals for bribery and high taxes. Only a return to kingly government, the three participants agree, can save the country.

Also early in 1648 Nedham may have been the author of <u>An Answer To a Declaration of the Lords and Commons</u>. Signed by "Mercurius Pragmaticus," it is clever enough to have called forth his talents for deception and, possibly in this instance, for self-deception. On January 11 Henry Marten, the most flamboyant and radical member of Parliament, published an attack on the Scottish Commissioners for their reactionary and anti-English propositions to the King.[22] "Pragmaticus" in his reply pretends to be a pro-English Scot--the only sort for whom Nedham would not hold his nose. This persona reviles Marten, refutes his arguments, and attacks the "Sectarian Army" for being greedy and tyrannical. He also questions religious toleration, somewhat ambiguously pointing out the contradiction between freedom of conscience and a Presbyterian settlement of the Church. The author seems reluctant to support Presbyterian orthodoxy, though he does state that "many Prophanations must inevitably follow" the granting of full religious toleration. An Answer To a Declaration concludes with only an indirect defense of the Scots: Parliament's own propositions to the King were "so destructive of his Majesties power, that we do not see how he could either in Conscience or Honour signe them." They were a trick, and now Parliament should "consider and repent."23

Shortly thereafter Nedham was responsible for a two-page tract, signed by him, which reprinted the Solemn League and Covenant of 1643 and the Negative Oath of 1647. The first was a pro-Presbyterian agreement between Parliament and the Scots, though to what it actually committed the signers continued to divide rather than unite them. The second was a promise never to bear arms against Parliament. On the eve of the Second Civil War, fought during the summer of 1648, Nedham needled the leaders of the army by his reminder of their earlier promises. His only contribution to The Solemn League and Covenant, besides the clever idea of reprinting it, was a short paragraph tacked on at the end:

Thus you may see how the inclination of the Disaffected Party were bent when this Covenant was made, and how solemnly it was taken by many of them....How near this comes to our times, I leave it to the Judicious Reader to judge, so that the ill consequences may be avoided.

In the first of two other pamphlets which Nedham wrote prior to the Second Civil War, The Manifold Practices and Attempts of the Hamiltons, he could resume being anti-Scot without besmirching his Royalist credentials. But this brief biography of James, First Duke of Hamilton, who led a Scottish army across the border in July, can more functionally be discussed in connection with Nedham's diatribe against him a year later: <u>Digitus Dei</u>. The second pamphlet by Nedham appeared in June, a month after <u>The Manifold Practises</u>. Signed by "Mercurius Pragmaticus" it is a short, clever, and nasty satire of a recent Lord Mayor of London: <u>The Reverend Alderman Atkins (The Shit-Breech) His Speech, to Mr. Warner the venerable Mayor of London</u>. Atkins was a favorite butt of Royalist jokes, most of them dealing with a public appearance at which he got so nervous he defecated in his pants. The title-page poem sets the tone for what follows:

> 'Twere pitie such a Speech as this should die,
> And not out-strip even Eternitie!
> So that after-ages may have knowledge,
> What revered Rulers once of Gotham Colledge,
> Sway'd famous London: Innocent indeed,
> For, most of them can neither write nor read.
> Fit underlings for Warner to advance,
> Who is himselfe the Prince of Ignorance.

Pragmaticus-Nedham then parodies Atkins' speech, including such malapropisms as the army returned home "augmented by the loss of 1,000 men," and he makes it obvious that Atkins, an ex-pimp and current Puritan, is stupid, greedy, hypocritical.[24]

But Nedham's chief occupation during the second half of 1648 remained the editing of <u>Mercurius Pragmaticus</u>. In August he bragged about "a deepe designe" being plotted against him by a member of the House of Commons, who allegedly announced in Parliament that <u>Pragmaticus</u> "comes abroad more exact and perfect than...ever...and relates all passages and whatever we say in the House and truly except some course be taken to prevent this.... I conceive we shall quite lose the freedom and privacy of our debates.... I suspect one of our own clerks, a drunken-debauched fellow with a red face."25 And in the same number Nedham boasted about his "Familiar" at Derby House, where the committee then ruling England held its meetings. Probably it was this red-faced alcoholic, not the Familiar, who supplied Nedham with this dramatic item:

> For the House being divided....and finding there were 57. on one side, and seven and fifty on the other, it was urged to Mr. Speaker that he should declare himself....Not knowing whether it were safe yet to quit the Army Faction, he paused a while and opened his mouth leisurely....

thereby, Nedham added, throwing a brief scare into the "Saints Vote-drivers."[26] Presumably an egg merchant whom Nedham accused of paying ₤60 for a seat in the House of Commons voted as he was instructed to.[27]

Nedham continued to display his political adroitness, though his performance became increasingly more difficult, dangerous, and hopeless. In July Pragmaticus was still openly, often bitterly, critical of the Presbyterians. In the autumn, after the defeat of the invading Scots, it became less hostile, and in November it praised the Presbyterian political program and leaders, though not their theology. He showed similar flexibility in regard to the Levellers. In the summer Nedham promoted a bout between good John Lilburne and bad Oliver Cromwell. In the fall he castigated the Levellers as the worst of rebels. Toward the end of the year he was equally bitter against them and the leaders of the army, though they can "as soon combine as fire and water...consider that the Levellers aim...at pure democracy, or a government of the many headed rabble, and the design of Oliver and His Grandees [is] for an Oligarchy in the hands of himself."[28]

Nedham had moved far from Mercurius Britanicus. The people are now "dregs," "the rascal Multitude," "the mob," "the Prophane vulgar." A stanza from a <u>Pragmaticus</u> title-page poem of late 1648 laments that:

> No god above, nor Gods below,
>   Our Saints (I see) will owne;
> Allegiance is Rebellion now,
>   Treason to weare a Crowne---

and Nedham goes on to explain, "Good God, what a wild thing is Rebellion!"[29]

During the final months of that year <u>Pragmaticus</u> was a sensitive barometer of the King's ups and downs--mainly his downs. As Charles's options narrowed, then disappeared, the weekly became even more strident and obviously distorted. Cromwell was, of course, the chief villain, and Nedham seemed to take delight in describing him as vulgar, bloodthirsty, hypocritical, power-mad, ugly. He called him, among other names, The Brewer, The Town Bull of Ely, King Cromwell, The Grand Segnior, Crum-Hell, Nose Almighty, Copper Nose. Nor did he hesitate to exploit a variety of wild anti-Cromwell rumors, especially stories about Cromwell and his stooges planning to cut off various designated heads in London. In a manner similar to that of <u>Mercurius Aulicus</u> in its final days, <u>Pragmaticus</u> minimized the New Model's victories in the Second Civil War and exaggerated as successes any skirmish in which the Royalists were not routed. During the ensuing negotiations between the victors and the King, Nedham depicted the former as Machiavellian subversives, the latter as a Christ-like martyr for English institutions. And he recurrently blamed the decay of trade--except, as he noted, that of preaching--on the "rebels."

As 1648 drew to a close, along with Charles's life, Cromwell and his colleagues tightened the censorship.[30] But for fifteen numbers, from August to mid-November, Nedham flouted the government by bringing <u>Pragmaticus</u> out in a twelve-page version. The last of these enlarged numbers, however, appeared after a gap of a week, with the censorial agents hot on Nedham's trail. Thereafter, for reasons of "security," the paper returned to its easier-to-print eight pages. Despite or because of these vicissitudes, <u>Pragmaticus</u> was salable enough to attract counterfeits, and at least five times between June and December another <u>Mercurius Pragmaticus</u> tried to cut into Nedham's market.[31] Then in January 1649, during the King's trial and execution, the army leaders, understandably fearful of the public reaction against these dramatic events, sent additional trackers into the alleys of London. No <u>Pragmaticus</u> appeared during the first three weeks of February, and Nedham himself had not covered the trial or the beheading of Charles I. He had temporarily jumped the Royalist ship, and the fortieth number of <u>Mercurius Pragmaticus</u>, covering the two weeks from December 26 to January 9, was either not the beneficiary of his deft touch or, at best, of only a small part of it.[32]

But his desertion of the King's cause was short-lived, and Nedham's sense of timing remained terrible. On November 30, two months before the King's execution, under the name "Pragmaticus," he published <u>A Plea for the King and Kingdome</u>. In October, Ireton, Cromwell's son-in-law, under pressure from the left had drawn up <u>The Remonstrance of the Army</u>. Essentially it made only two points: first, that by inviting the Scots to invade England Charles had proved that he wanted almost absolute power and that, consequently, further negotiations with him would be futile; second, that it was both expedient and just that he be brought to trial—and condemned. Nedham, in desperate rebuttal, could again only try to divide the King's enemies. <u>A Plea</u> is addressed to the House of Commons, and part of its sub-title announces that it will prove that <u>The Remonstrance of the Army</u> "tends to subvert the Lawes and fundamental Constitutions of the Kingdom, and demolish the very Foundations of Government in generall." Nedham prefaces his twenty-page detailed and quibbling refutation of Ireton by asserting that <u>The Remonstrance</u> is an "affront" to

Parliament from the army: "Do they [the army] not challenge you [the House of Commons] as inconstant to your own Votes and Resolutions, perfidious to that trust reposed in you?"

As Nedham knew, it was a lost cause; but after much sparring, in his concluding paragraph he goes down swinging:

> Many more instances might be given, but none more pat than these for the present occasion; wherein (as in a glass) every man may behold those fatall miseries and confusions, that must needs ensue a change of the Kingly to a popular, or (as the case now stands with us) to a Military Government; which I have proved clearly unto the world to be the designe of this Remonstrance, to the utter subversion of our Law, the fundamental constitutions and Priviledges of Parliament, with the destruction of the king and his Posterity, and the inslaving of the Kingdome....And if any of you should miscarry, and be purged out of the House (as some of you [e.g., the eleven members whom Prynne had defended and Nedham attacked] have been heretofore by this Faction) and forced to banishment, it will be your chiefest glory in time to come, that you suffered in behalf of your King and Country.

Nedham was being prophetic for both the short and the long run. A week after A Plea appeared, Colonel Pride purged the House of Commons of those Members who opposed the army. Within a month Nedham went into hiding.

This was the right place to be. In late January a London weekly reported that "Pragmaticus"--Nedham's successor--had been arrested.[33] This successor or another one (jail terms were usually short and escapes could be arranged) in February dramatically announced that he had been "routed out of his lodgings...by Parliament beagles and whole squadrons of rebellious Mermidons,

& forc't to build his nest in another angle."[34] Wood reports that at this period Nedham, "being narrowly sought after, left London, and for a time sculk'd at Minster Lovel near Burford...in the house of Dr. Pet. Heylyn."[35] Heylyn was actually then living in the house of his elder brother,[36] to which Nedham fled, but this does not undercut the fact that politics makes strange bedfellows.

Sometime in the early spring of 1649 Nedham returned to London. He probably lent a hand to the sporadic Royalist weeklies that were sniping at the new Commonwealth. In March he reputedly sent two secret "letters of intelligence" to Charles II in France.[37] On April 9 he re-entered the public arena with the publication of Digitus Dei. This pamphlet included Nedham's most brilliant literary work, an Epitaph on the Duke of Hamilton, which momentarily raises Nedham to the level of a much more famous turncoat, John Dryden.

Hilary Rubinstein, the modern biographer of James, First Duke of Hamilton, aptly entitles her book, Captain Luckless.[38] Hamilton was ambitious, devious, fickle, inept--and unlucky. Peter Heylyn describes him as a "notable dissembler, true only to his own ends, and a most excellent master in the art of insinuation."[39] Neither Bishop Burnet's eulogistic account in 1673 nor Clarendon's attempt to paint a favorable portrait do much to rehabilitate him.[40] During the 1640's he managed at one time or another to be reviled by all political factions, often by several concurrently. Nedham, writing from a Royalist point of view, illustrates this, despite the fact that on March 9, 1649 Hamilton was beheaded by the Commonwealth government.

In May 1648 Nedham wrote The Manifold Practises and Attempts of the Hamiltons, And particularly of the present Duke of Hamilton...To Get the Crown of Scotland. In a generally circumstantial narrative Nedham tries to show that for 120 years the Hamiltons have aimed at the Scottish throne, and that since 1641 the First Duke's scramble for regal power has been frantic and duplicituous. For instance: in 1643 he "thought it time for him to passe over from the Covenanters and pretend for the King, that by having access to his counsels, he might betray them." Or: In 1648 Hamilton and his cronies "kept of[f] the King with faire pretences from coming to Scotland...and within a few days he was delivered over to the Parliaments Commissioners." Near the end of his twenty-three-page account Nedham sardonically concludes that, "I make no question, but if the Duke could be king of Scotland, his tender conscience might, without the help of Divines, be persuaded to digest with a moderate Episcopacie, though we love not to buy at that rate. How Absalom like do they court the people with pretences for good of Religion, King and Kingdomes; as if they intended nothing, but to performe their vows in Hebron?"[41]

Hamilton had long been a Royalist--one whom Nedham had occasionally attacked in Mercurius Britanicus. As editor of Pragmaticus, though he briefly praised Hamilton when he led a disorganized Scottish army into England, Nedham again assailed the luckless Duke. The most dramatic example occurs in one of the final numbers in mid-December: reporting Cromwell's efforts to get Hamilton to save his life by squealing on his accomplices, Nedham writes, "It's thought the cunning coward (for as yet we cannot call him traitor) has told tales." Later in the same number he adds that, despite "much discourse," Hamilton has not yet talked.[42]

Then in April, a month after Hamilton's execution, Nedham published Digitus Dei: Or, God's Justice upon Treachery and Treason; Exemplified in the Life and Death of the late James Duke of Hamilton. Being an exact Relation of his Traiterous practises since the Year 1630. Together with a true and full Discovery of the mysteries of his last Engagement for the destruction of the

<u>King, and his Royall Posterity. Whereto is added an Epitaph</u>. The prose in this thirty-two-page pamphlet is crisp and functional, and the Epitaph is, I think, the finest satiric elegy of the Interregnum.

Nedham's relatively terse recapitulation of Hamilton's career indicates how he managed to get himself hated by almost all factions in England and Scotland. What follows is a small sampling:

1630: Hamilton "came speedily to the King, who at first entertained him, not with the familiarity he was wont: But by his cunning insinuations he soon prevailed over the King's good nature."

1631: "He increased his faction in the English Court, placing creatures of his own, nearest the King, even in his Bed-chamber, kept constant correspond with the Presbyters in Scotland, cajoled the Bishops here, and cut their throats underhand."

late 1630's: He was "a Pensioner of the French King, and . . . received Advice and Instructions from . . . Cardinal Richelieu."

ca. 1640: "By his usual sleights he crept again in to the most gracious Kings Counsels and Favour, and became Intelligencer to Pym and his Faction."

1643: He "plaied a new part in Scotland in pretending highly for the King, that having access again to his Counsels he might betray them."

ca. 1645: "He left his Brethren of Independency in the lurch, and fell off from Argile."

Late 1648: "Cromwell sent his Beagles to bait him; and, with others, in come Buffone [Hugh Peters] ...with open mouth, Oho my Lord that you should be so treacherous and deceitfull, as to invade your friends in England."

1649: He was "condemned to the Block, a sacrifice to the revenge of this Faction [the army] for his former jugling, and to the jealousie of Argile, and the Kirke of Scotland."

It is a dark portrait. But in a Postscript Nedham lightens it by making Cromwell and the other executioners of Hamilton seem even darker:

> It is to be noted, that they kept Hamilton in hope of life to the very last moment, for feare he should give glory to God, and throw shame and infamy upon themselves, by an ingenious confession of his own, Argile's, and their mutual vilanies. Besides, such a discovery would have made Argile less serviceable to them in Scotland; whose next designe is to Cajole the Kirke, by dis-avowing any the least correspond with the Sectaries of England, and putting on new pretences of serving the Presbyterian interest.
> Be it known too, that when the 3 Lords [Hamilton, Holland, Capel] were murther'd upon that Stage of Tyranny, Cromwell,...and divers others of the savage crew stood in a room belonging to the Star-Chamber, scoffing, and triumphing in the ruine of the Nobility; and made use of perspective-glasses, that they might feed their eyes with those bloody Spectacles.

But in the Epitaph Nedham uses a rapier, not a bludgeon:

> He that three Kingdomes made one flame,
> Blasted their beauty, burn't the frame,
> Himself now here in ashes lies
> A part of this great Sacrifice.
> Here all of HAMILTON remains,
> Save what the other world contains.
> But (Reader) it is hard to tell
> Whether that world be Heav'n or Hell.
> A Scotch man enters Hell at's birth
> And 'scapes it when he goes to earth,

Assur'd no worse a Hell can come
Than that which he enjoy'd at home.
   How did the Royal Workman botch
This Duke, halfe-English, and halfe-
  Scotch:
A Scot an English Earldom fits,
As Purple doth your Marmuzets;
Suits like Nol Cromwell with the Crown,
Or Bradshaw in his Scarlet-gown.
Yet might he thus disguis'd (no lesse)
Have slip't to Heav'n in's English dresse,
But that he in hope of life became
[a line is here missing]....
This mystick Proteus too as well
Might cheat the Devill, 'scape his Hell,
Since to those pranks he pleas'd to play,
Religion ever pav'd the way;
Which he did to a Faction tie,
Not to reforme, but crucifie.
'Twas he that first alarm'd the Kirke
To this prepost'rous bloody worke,
Upon the Kings to place Christs Throne,
A step, and foot-stoole to his owne;
Taught Zeale a hundred tumbling tricks.
And Scriptures twin'd with Politicks;
The Pulpit made a Jugler-Box,
Set Law and Gospell in the Stocks,
As did old Buchanan and Knox,
In those daies when (at once) the Pox
And Presbyters a way did find
Into the World, to plague mankind.
'Twas he patch's up the new Divine,
Part Calvin, and part Cataline,
Could too trans-forme (without a Spell)
Satan into a Gabriel;
Just like those pictures which we paint
On this side Fiend, on that side Saint.
Both this, and that, and ev'rything
He was; for, and against the King;
Rather than he his ends would misse,
Betray'd his Master with a kisse,
And buri'd in one common Fate
The glory of our Church and State;
The Crown too levell'd on the ground;
And having rock't all parties round,

>'Faith, it was time then to be gone,
> Since he had all his business done.
>   Next, on the fatall Block expir'd,
> He to this Marble-Cell retir'd;
> Where all of HAMILTON remains
> But what Eternity contains.[43]

Digitus Dei reported, as we have seen, that among the cronies of Cromwell who bullied Hamilton at the end was Hugh Peters, an exuberant Independent minister whom Nedham had praised in 1646 in *Independencie No Schisme* and subsequently attacked in *Pragmaticus*. Now late in April 1649 he cleverly parodied Cromwell's then favorite clergyman in a *Most Pithy Exhortation Delivered in an Eloquent Oration To The Watry Generation Aboard Their Admirall at Graves-end. By the Right Reverend, Mr. Hugh Peters, Doctor of the Chair for the famous University of Whitehall, and Chaplain in ordinary to the High and Mighty K. Oliver, the first of that name, as it was took, verbatim, in short hand (when he delivered it).*[44] Nedham captures the heartiness and cockiness of the Right Reverend: for example, "Y'have as good beer aboard, as ever wet whistle; Colonel Pride [a former brewer] can give ye an account of more grains and hops spent in the brewing on't, than his belly will hold"; or, "I think the Parliament has took as great care for your [the sailors'] temporal food, as for your spiritual diet, or else they ne're have sent me hither to preach such crums of comfort to ye." Peters promises to get the admirals' names memorialized in Hebrew so that "their fames may be read backwards," and he taunts the sailors for leaving behind them wives who will promptly prove unfaithful.

Concurrent with this short and relatively lighthearted bit of mockery, Nedham returned to being a Royalist editor, now of *Mercurius Pragmaticus (For King Charles II)*. Again during the spring and summer of 1649 the skein of the Royalist press, though involving many fewer weeklies than a year earlier, is tangled: journals changed names and editors, publication was sporadic, imitation and borrowing frequent. The stringency of the censorship varied. It was loose in May, then grew steadily tighter until by mid-1650 only one of approximately a dozen weeklies survived. <u>Mercurius Pragmaticus</u>, with a variety of editors, among them John Cleveland, and skipping many weeks, hung on until almost as long.[45] Nedham, however, hung on as editor for only two months. In June 1649 he found himself in jail.

In the first number of his revived <u>Pragmaticus</u> Nedham announced that "here comes old Prag. himself new mounted."[46] He had not lost his touch. In late April he portrayed Robert Lockyer, a Leveller who was executed for mutiny and whose London funeral drew a huge and sympathetic crowd, as a "Martyr for the Liberties of England."[47] In May he criticized a new Treason Act with arguments that anticipate those of John Stuart Mill.[48] He retained his skill in dramatizing contrasts: the pomp of Whitehall versus the poverty of the exiled Charles II; or, "betwixt the two Factions we shall never be at rest; for all the week we are slaves to the Independents, and on Sunday to the Presbyter."[49] In the ninth and final number written by him, covering the week of June 12 to 19, Nedham wound up his career as a Royalist journalist with a sentimental account of how the blood of the dead King had cured the eyes of a young girl, and with several cynical references to New England as a sanctuary for the Grandees when they would be forced to flee from old England.

On June 15 the Council of State ordered the Sergeant at Arms to apprehend Marchamont Nedham, "the author of Pragmaticus, and other libels, and seize his books and papers."[50] A few days later he was captured and sent to Newgate, where, says Wood cryptically, he was "brought into danger of his life."[51] Wood was soon proved eminently wrong. Instead of executing Nedham, the government hired him. He did stay in Newgate for five months, except for two weeks in August when he escaped.[52] But by the middle of November 1649 he had arranged to buy his freedom with those talents which were metaphorical death for him to hide. He was ready to go to work for Crum-Hell, The Town Bull of Ely, old Copper Nose.

Footnotes   Chapter III

1. Wood, p. 1181. Wood dates Nedham's becoming a doctor in 1645. Possibly he is a year early, though I am strongly inclined to agree with him. Nedham later seems to date the beginning of his practice of medicine in 1645.

2. See below, pp. 108-110.

3. Knachel, *Case*, p. xxi; Wood, p. 1184.

4. Signed "By a Lover of Truth, Peace and Honesty," this point-by-point refutation of *The Case* appeared in July 1647. The author's stance is mildly pro-Presbyterian. One passage pays an unintended compliment to Nedham's effectiveness: "and truly the Independent interest is notably acted in this Booke, which is but a dramaticall representation of Independency, which is here set forth, painted with wit and words, crying out, *Who is on my side, who?* nay represented so glorious, that all sides must wooe her, as though none can stand or flourish without her friendship."

5. For the factual background of the Civil War and then of the Commonwealth and Protectorate I rely heavily on Samuel Rawson Gardiner, *History of the Great Civil War*, 4 vols., London: Longmans, Green, and Co., 1893, and *History of the Commonwealth and Protectorate*, 4 vols., London: Longmans Green, and Co., 1903; and on Charles Harding Firth, *The Last Years of the Protectorate*, 2 vols., London: Longmans, Green, and Co., 1909. Godfrey Davis, *The Restoration of Charles II, 1658-1660*, San Marino: The Huntington Library, 1955, completes this splendid coverage of the Interregnum. For the intellectual ferment of this period, I have learned much from three books by

Christopher Hill: *The World Turned Upside Down*, London: Temple Smith, 1972; *Change and Continuity in Seventeenth-Century England*, London: Weidenfeld and Nicholsen, 1974; and *Milton and the English Revolution*, New York: The Viking Press, 1977.

6. Wood, p. 1181. The date of this meeting, though Wood does not specify it, is early September. Charles was brought to Hampton Court late in August, and the first number of *Mercurius Pragmaticus* appeared on Sept. 21.

7. Wood, p. 1181.

8. Frank, *BN*, p. 142.

9. Frank, *BN*, pp. 139, 143ff.

10. Frank, *BN*, p. 139.

11. Firth, *DNB*.

12. Frank, *BN*, p. 139.

13. Frank, *BN*, passim.

14. Frank, *BN*, p. 333; *Mercurius Pragmaticus*, no. 12, Nov. 30-Dec. 7, 1647. Firth, *DNB* points out that *Pragmaticus* was frequently quoted by the compilers of the 'Old Parliamentary History.'

15. Frank, *BN*, p. 141, *Prag.*, no. 3, Sept. 28-Oct. 6, 1647; no. 6, Oct. 19-26, 1647; no. 9, Nov. 9-16, 1647; no. 11, Nov. 23-30, 1647; no. 17, Jan. 4-11, 1648; no. 18, Jan. 18-25, 1648; no. 23, Feb. 15-25, 1648; no. 28, March 21-28, 1648, no. 1 (in a new series) March 28-April 4, 1648; no. 5, Apr. 25-May 2, 1648; no. 6, May 2-9, 1648; no. 12, June 13-20, 1648; no. 26, Sept. 19-26, 1648; no. 27, Sept. 26-Oct. 3, 1648; no. 30, Oct. 17-24, 1648.

16. *Prag.*, no. 14, Feb. 24-March 3, 1648; no. 28, March 21-28, 1648. H.N. Brailsford, <u>The Levellers and the English Revolution</u>, London: The Cresset press, 1961, pp. 488f. finds *Pragmaticus* more sympathetic to the Levellers than I think the evidence warrants.

17. *Prag.*, no. 5, Oct. 12-20, 1647.

18. *Prag.*, no. 4, oct. 5-12, 1647.

19. *Prag.*, no. 6, Oct. 19-26, 1647.

20. *Prag.*, no. 6 (new series), March 14-21, 1648.

21. Two similar short dramas appeared in 1648, both signed by "Mercurius Melancholicus": <u>Craftie Cromwell: Or Oliver ordering our New State</u>, and <u>Mistris Parliament Presented in her Bed, after some travaile...in the birth of her Monstrous Offspring</u>. In message and style they are similar to <u>The Levellers levell'd</u>, but Wood does not attribute them to Nedham and the name "Pragmaticus" does not appear in connection with either of them.

22. <u>The Independency of England endeavored to be maintained by Henry Marten...against the Claim of the Scottish Commissioners</u>.

23. The poor job of printing this pamphlet suggests that it was published hastily and surreptitiously.

24. Thomas Atkins served as Sheriff in London in 1637-38, as an Alderman from 1638 to 1661, and as Lord Mayor in 1644-45. He was a moderate Independent in his politics, but was mainly interested in business, and he succeeded in well feathering his own nest. I cannot verify the historicity of the "shit-breech" anecdote. (For further details see

Pearl, London and the Outbreak of the Puritan Revolution, pp. 311-13.

25. Prag., no. 21, Aug. 15-22, 1648.

26. Prag., no. 18, July 25-Aug. 1, 1648. This is not the first reference to party whips. Mercurius Britanicus, five years earlier, had implied that Pym used them when necessary.

27. Prag., no. 19, Aug. 1-8, 1648.

28. Prag., no. 39, Dec. 19-26, 1648.

29. Prag., no. 35, Nov. 21-28j, 1648.

30. This tightening of the censorship, however, was neither sudden nor unexpected. As early as January 1648 the House of Commons "ordered [that] the Committee concerning the suppressing Scandalous and Unlicensed Pamphlets should meet daily, and take special care for preventing any such to come out for the future....[and that] a Sum of Money...be paid unto the said Committee, to gratify some that had lately discovered where the Presses of some Malignant sheets were: and to gratify such as shall make any Discovery of the Authors or Presses of such malignant and abusive Sheets." (John Rushworth, Historical Collections, The Second Edition, London, 1721, Part IV, Vol. II, p. 957.) At the end of the year Nedham and his colleagues were merely in considerably greater danger than they had been at its start.

31. Frank, BN, p. 162.

32. Nedham later acknowledged that he retired after this number of Mercurius Pragmaticus [Mercurius Pragmaticus (For King Charles II), no. 1, April 17-24, 1649]; even so, his connection with no. 40 was almost certainly minimal.

33. *Perfect Occurrences*, no. 108, Jan. 19-26, 1649.

34. *Prag.*, no. 43, Feb. 20-27, 1649.

35. Wood, p. 1181.

36. See the article on Heylyn by Mandell Creighton in *DNB*.

37. David Underdown, *Royalist Conspiracy in England 1649-1660*, New Haven: Yale University Press, 1960, p. 22.

38. Hilary L. Rubinstein, *Captain Luckless - James, First Duke of Hamilton 1606-1649*, Edinburgh: Scottish Academic Press, 1975.

39. From one of the epigraphs in Rubinstein, *Captain Luckless*.

40. Gilbert Burnet, *The Memoirs of the Lives and Actions of James and William, Dukes of Hamilton...*, London, 1673: reprinted Oxford, at the Oxford University press, 1852. Clarendon's summary of Hamilton in his *History of the Rebellion and Civil Wars* is given in Rubenstein, *Captain Luckless*, p. 245.

41. In July 1648 *The Lier laid open....* attempted to reply to Nedham.

42. *Prag.*, no. 38, Dec. 12-19, 1648.

43. A satire published in 1659, a decade after Hamilton's death (and a decade after the Cromwellian government, fearing he might become a martyr, confiscated and then destroyed a variety of materials pertaining to his life and execution), showed that he was still widely unpopular. It concluded:
    A traitor I lived, and a traitor I died,
    And yet with both parties I never complied;

> 'Tis strange, you will say, but here is the reason,
> I true was to neither, so suffered for treason.

(Quoted in Rubinstein, *Captain Luckless*, p. 243.

44. For the dating of this pamphlet, see Raymond Stearns, *The Strenous Puritan: Hugh Peter 1598-1660*, Urbana: University of Illinois Press, 1454, p. 344.

45. Frank, *BN*, pp. 192f.

46. *Mercurius Pragmaticus (For King Charles II)*, no. 1, Apr. 17-24, 1649. The editor of *Mercurius Pragmaticus, For King Charles II*, no. 1, Sept. 10-17, 1649, comments that he is not "the former editor of *Britanicus*" who had "usurped" the name Pragmaticus.

47. *Mercurius Pragmaticus (For King Charles II)*, no. 1, Sept. 10-17, 1649.

48. *Mercurius Pragmaticus (For King Charles II)*, no. 3, May 1-8, 1649.

49. *Mercurius Pragmaticus (For King Charles II)*, no. 7, May 29-June 5, 1649; no. 8, June 5-12, 1649.

50. *Calendar of State Papers, Domestic*, 1649-50, p. 537.

51. Wood, p. 1181.

52. J. Milton French, "Milton, Nedham, and 'Mercurius Politicus'," *Studies in Philology*, XXVI (1936), 236. The evidence for his escape is an order, dated Aug. 14, that he be rearrested (*Calendar of State Papers, Domestic*, 1649-50, p. 507.

CHAPTER IV

THIRD MOVEMENT--1649-1660

The first step Nedham took toward a new deal was the publication, early in August 1649, of a signed pamphlet: <u>Certain Considerations Tendered in all humility, to an honorable Member of the Council of State</u>.[1] He begins by referring to his six weeks in prison and to his thoughts on censorship during this period of enforced idleness. Then in five short sections he indirectly pleads his own case, with a rare touch of humility and an outpouring of classical allusions. First, a new government should be merciful and whenever possible avoid harshness. Second, it is expedient for a new government to allow some freedom of speech. Third, it is also expedient for that new government to take a "negative carriage" toward "pasquils," though often they should be "below the care and consideration of men in Authority." But fourth, the situation is far otherwise with attacks on the government from the pulpit. Citing ancient and modern threats from "Pulpit-Politicians" like Savonarola, Nedham advocates state control of preaching. Fifth, he attacks the use of informers--"secret whisperers"--because they are a demoralizing influence and they are usually crooked and ambitious.

Apparently Nedham was not sanguine about any immediate rewards for his judicious and learned <u>Considerations</u>, and he promptly managed to escape from Newgate. But by the middle of the month he was captured and brought back. Nedham should have been more optimistic. As Wood explains, "Lenthall the speaker of the house of commons who knew him and his relations well, and John Bradshaw, president of the high court of justice, treated him fairly, and not only got his pardon, but, with promise of rewards and places, persuaded him to change his stile once more, meaning for the independents, then carrying all before them."[2] Presumably this persuasion was not difficult, though it may have taken some time to work out the details concerning rewards and places.

Early in November Nedham signed the Engagement to be loyal to the Commonwealth, and on November 14 he was released from Newgate.[3] Lenthall and Brandshaw probably first propositioned him in September.[4] This could not have been easy for them. Both had been virulently attacked in Pragmaticus, and in April Digitus Dei had called Bradshaw "that monster" and described the court which tried Charles I and over which he presided as "the most absolute stage of tyranny and injustice that ever was in the world."

In return for his freedom, along with the promise of a high salary, Nedham offered to write a lengthy pamphlet in support of the new Commonwealth and to edit a pro-government newspaper. In May 1650 The Case of the Commonwealth of England, Stated appeared; in June the first number of Mercurius Politicus was for sale in London. In between, on May 24, the Council of State ordered that "₤100 yearly be paid by Mr. Frost [the Secretary of the Council] to Marchamont Nedham as a pension, whereby he may subsist while endeavoring to serve the Commonwealth; this to be done for one year, by way of probation....Mr. Frost to pay him also ₤50 as a gift for service already done."[5] This was a large sum of money; and a seat at or very near the center of power was a long way from a cell in Newgate. Nedham had made a very good deal.

Lenthall and Bradshaw had taken the initiative, perhaps prodded by some of Nedham's colleagues from his days as editor of Mercurius Britanicus. But Nedham's greatest asset was his reputation as an effective propagandist. He was a true professional in both senses of the word: he had mastered the skills of his trade, and he did not come cheap. The next decade proved that Lenthall and Bradshaw, not to mention Cromwell, had also made a very good deal.

The Case of the Commonwealth is Nedham's most unified, most thoughtful, and most persuasive work. Moreover, its sustained Hobbesian approach to political theory is still alarmingly pertinent. Fortunately The Case has been reprinted by the Folger Shakespeare Library, expertly edited by Philip Knachel. He and I agree that it is worthy of study and analysis.

Since early 1649, as Mercurius Pragmaticus had recurrently noted--and gloated--the new government had to face the problem of its own legitimacy. One solution was some kind of loyalty oath, and for almost a year debate in Parliament and print crescendoed about the efficacy and morality of such an "Engagement," as well as about its form and who should take it.[6] At first it was only mandatory for high officials of the government and Members of Parliament to "declare and promise that [they] will be true and faithful to the Commonwealth of England, as it is now established, without a King or House of Lords." In October 1649 this oath was extended to members of the army, ministers, and a variety of local officials. Finally, early in 1650 it was broadened to include every English male over eighteen, and Parliament directed that the courts should refuse justice to all persons who did not take this Engagement. The one amendment which the Commons accepted was proposed by Henry Marten: it exempted women by substituting "men" for "persons" in the enacting clause. Marten's argument that "though they baited the bull, they would not bait the cow too" was a rare touch of humor amid the flood of serious polemics.[7]

Nedham was fully aware of these current polemics engendered by the Engagement Controversy, and he had read much of the relevant literature of political theory from the preceding 2,000 years. In 1649 and 1650 that controversy spawned a large number of persuasive and thoughtful treatises, representing all shades of opinion; collectively they demonstrate that English political thought could be extremely sophisticated--and modern. But

Nedham's title, <u>The Case of the Commonwealth</u>, was not intended to suggest, say, Aristotle or Machiavelli or Bodin, but to recall his own <u>The Case of the Kingdom</u> of 1647; and the title-page is modeled on that of the earlier tract. Nedham begins the short prefactory "To the Reader" with the deadpan admission:

> Perhaps thou art of an opinion contrary to what is here written. I confess that for a time I myself was so too, till some causes made me reflect with an impartial eye upon the affairs of the new government....I know the high talkers, the lighter censorious part of people, will shoot many a bitter arrow to wound my reputation and charge me with levity and inconstancy because I am not obstinate like themselves against conscience, right reason, necessity, the custom of all nations, and the peace of our own.[8]

This was no breast-beating confession. Rather, it was a ploy that was at once unavoidable and clever: unavoidable because Nedham's two-year allegiance to the Royalist cause had been highly visible and audible; clever because if he could change his mind, so could other opponents of the new government.

The 100-page <u>Case of the Commonwealth</u> is divided into two parts, the first directed to "the conscientious man," the second to "the worldling." "The former will approve nothing but what is just and equitable.... The latter will embrace anything, so it make for his profit."[9]

Part I, Chapter I- 'That Governments Have Their Revolutions and Fatal Periods' - harks back to Polybius and anticipates the theory of Vico and such novelists as Conrad and Joyce. History is cyclical. All governments are born, grow, and die. No government lasts indefinitely, regardless of its worth. Nedham cites many examples from classical and modern history to support this view.
"No wonder then if our English monarchy, having

arrived to almost six hundred years since the Conquest, should now, according to the common fate of all other governments, resign up her interest to some other power, family, or form." And he cynically concludes: "When all is done, we shall find it but labor in vain, that we have but fortified castles in the air against fatal necessity to maintain a fantasy of pretended loyalty;...how foolishly we have hazarded our lives and fortunes and sacrificed the lives of others with the common good and peace of the nation for the satisfying of an opinionated humor."[10]

Chapter 2- 'That the Power of the Sword Is, and Ever Hath been, the Foundation of All Titles to Government' - is central to Nedham's argument, and this concept does much to explain his role for the rest of the 1650's. Again he profusely cites historical sources, and now the Bible, to confirm his hypothesis. Among many examples are the Thirty Years War, in which "One while, you might have seen the same town under the French, the next under the Spaniard. And upon every new alteration, without scruple, paying a new allegiance and submission, and never so much as blamed for it by the divines of their own or any other nation."[11] Indeed all governments originally had "no other dependence than upon the sword." Then the peroration:

> Whosoever therefore shall refuse submission to an established government upon pretense of conscience in regard of former allegiance, oaths, and covenants, or upon supposition that it is by the sword unlawfully erected, deserves none but the character of peevish, and a man obstinate against the reason and custom of the whole world. Let his pretense be what it will, resistance, in the eye of the law of nations, is treason; and if he will needs perish in the flames of his own phrenetic zeal, he can at the best be reckoned but the madman's saint and the fool's martyr.[12]

The events of the last 330 years have confirmed this hardboiled thesis. In 1650 it could appeal to the Royalists and Presbyterians for two reasons. First, it took them off a moral hook in that they did not have to justify the new government, merely to accept its existence. Second, it assumed that history is not only amoral, it is also non-Providential. Thus the army's victory was not necessarily a sign of God's blessing on his saints, as Milton and many Independents believed, but a result that could be explained by secular causes. Being on the losing side, therefore, was not an indication that one was a sinner, merely that he had showed poor judgment, made a bad bet.

The short third chapter- 'That Nonsubmission to Government Justly Deprives Men of the Benefit of Its Protection'- "proves" that both the Law of God and the Law of Nature are against anarchy and that they demand obedience to de facto authority. "It is ground enough for the submission of particular persons in things of political equity that those which have gotten the power are irresistible and able to force it if they refuse."[13] Chapter IV is equally Hobbesian: 'That a Government Erected by a Prevailing Part of the People Is As Valid de jure As If It Had the Ratifying Consent of the Whole.' One chilling passage can epitomize Nedham's logic and learning:

> Warlike acquisitions hold as good in civil divisions within the same nation as in war betwixt nation and nation. For where a nation is engaged in a civil war and divided into parties, the eye of the law of nations looks not on them as one nation, but as two, according to that of Grotius: <u>In regno diviso, gens una, pro tempore, quasi duae gentens habentur</u>, "In a divided state one nation during the time of its national divisions is esteemed as two nations"; so that what pre-eminence nation may gain over nation by right of foreign war, the same may be obtained likewise by one part of a nation

against the other by right of civil war. And what the foreign conqueror may do in changing the government, abolishing old laws and establishing new, the same may be done also by the civil victor for his own security.[14]

Chapter 5 is entitled 'That the Oath of Allegiance and the Covenant Are No Justifiable Grounds to Raise a New War in, or against, the Commonwealth of England.' Again Nedham tries intellectually to disarm the Royalists and Presbyterians: they will not be renegades if they accept the new powers-that-be.

As for the Oath of Allegiance: in a word, allegiance is but a political tie for politic ends, grounded upon political considerations; and therefore, being politically determined, when those considerations are altered by new circumstances (be it in relation to Caesar or the Senate) the old allegiance is extinct and must give place to a new. The same description may serve likewise for the Covenant. For even that part of it which relates most to religion will be found wrapped up altogether in matters of discipline and church polity to serve politic ends and interests, if the actions of our English and Scotch Presbyters may be admitted as a comment upon the text. I grant, both those oaths are religious acts as they are solemnized with the invocation of God as a witness. But as all actions are qualified from their principal end, so the main end of those oaths being obedience to the prince in order to the good of the public, they are of a political nature. and when such an alteration of affairs shall happen as extinguishes his title, I conceive we are not obliged, in this case, to pay him that submission which by oath we promised but ought rather to swear a new one to those that succeed him in the government.[15]

The second part of The Case is twice as long as the first. Nedham was more interested in application than theory--and even when he was theorizing he kept his eye fixed on the political scene. In terms of "utility" rather than "equity" he goes on to show that the Royalists, Presbyterians, and Levellers are each unable to defeat the new regime, and that it is in the long-range interest of each not to fight a losing battle. The Scots he handles differently.

First, the Royalists. Charles II can expect no aid from abroad, and no significant help from Scotland and Ireland. Nor can he anticipate a successful uprising in England. But should the King succeed against these overwhelming odds, his restoration would result in so much bloodshed and bitterness that he could only rule as a tyrant. Nedham's concluding sentence to this lengthy chapter is predictable and patronizing:

> I may undeniably conclude that all mistaken Royalists, as well as others, who now live under the protection of the present government are concerned out of necessity and in respect to their own well-being and benefit to wish well thereunto rather than prosecute the private interest of a single family and of a few fugitives, its dependents, to the hazard of their own families, with the peace and happiness of their native country.[16]

In the next chapter, 'Concerning the Scots,' Nedham releases his long-held but recently suppressed dislike of them. He begins: "I am sorry I must waste paper upon this nation."[17] Then somewhat in the manner of Digitus Dei he recounts the history of their "profane projects," which have reached the point where now "no man that is master of an English spirit but will abhor the hypocritical pretenses and encroachments of that perfidious nation."[18] Nedham is here vehement and bitter, but he can also be wry and sardonic--for instance:

Let me call to mind a story of the hedgehog in the fable who being almost dead with cold chanced to light upon a fox's kennel; where, asking for entertainment, the fox, more compassionate than wise, grants his request. But the hedgehog, as soon as he recovered warmth, began to bristle and prick the fox; who, complaining of his unworthy carriage, the hedgehog made answer that if he found him troublesome, he might leave him and seek a new lodging. I shall make no application but leave those that would entertain the Scots as their friends to consider whether they should find more courtesy from them if they had power here than the fox did from the hedgehog ....[19]

Because the Scots are beyond the pale, Nedham does not deal with their self-interest. But it is to the interest of all Englishmen to "abhor" Scottish interference in their affairs, whether by preacher or politician.

Nedham is almost as negative in his treatment of the English Presbyterians. Again he utilizes history to try to prove his case. Though he recurrently cites the Bible and occasionally the Will of God, his tone is irreverent, sometimes mocking. Nothing in Hobbes surpasses the flippant quality of this paragraph from Nedham's short history of Presbyterianism.

It was no sooner licked into form there [Geneva] but, as it is the fate of all things new, it began to be much extolled and admired; and the fame thereof, spreading in England as well as other parts, wrought in many of our countrymen an itching desire to go thither and instruct themselves in the nature and customs of the government. Where, of spectators, they soon become proselytes and, returning home with new affections, looked with an eye of disdain upon the bishops; as if themselves had indeed found out the pattern in the Mount because forsooth the words presbytery, elder, deacon, & assembly, &c., sound more gospellike than diocese, churchwarden, archdeacon, and high commission, &c. With these terms, the ordinary sort of religious persons, not able to see through this shell of words into the kernel or substance of the business, were easily led to a belief of high matters; whereas this new form, like the Trojan horse, brought an army of mischiefs in the belly of it, which were never so fully discovered as till this Parliament. For immediately after that episcopal form was abolished here, as corrupt and antichristian, the chief sticklers of the presbyterian clergy began to show their teeth and, sitting in an assembly cheek by jowl with the parliament, intermeddled with their affairs, labored to twist their church discipline with the interest of state, claimed in their open pleas, discourses, and their confession of faith a power in themselves distinct from the civil, and demanded the voting of this in both Houses as <u>jure divino</u> that so the Parliament might forever cut the throat of their own authority and magistracy.[20]

Because of their dismal record and current unpopularity, the Presbyterians cannot succeed in their anti-Commonwealth designs. Even the Royalists are vindictive against them, because "though they laid him [Charles I] not down upon the block, yet they brought him to the scaffold."[21] Moreover, every Englishman should be wary of Presbyterian intolerance, which would force "all the people...like asses to be ridden by them and their arbitrary assemblies."[22] The Presbyterian cause is doomed to fail, and reasonable men, including reasonable Presbyterians, will find it in their self-interest to support the Commonwealth.

Despite his defense of religious toleration and of a government without King or House of Lords, Nedham adopts a strongly anti-democratic position 'Concerning the Levellers.' He begins with a brief history of the Leveller movement since 1647, a movement which started well but quickly degenerated. He is particularly negative about their proposed Agreement of the People of May 1649. Nedham refers to this democratic constitution as a "perfidious" design, a "wild project," a "hopefull way to...satisfy their natural appetites of covetousness and revenge," etc. This is the first of ten anti-Leveller "arguments." He next attacks the concept of democracy which permeates the Agreement. The rule of the people can only lead to the tyranny of the "hot-headed rabble," then to that of a restored monarchy. Nedham's third argument is the prospect of "what tumults and combustions needs must happen every year by reason of those prodigious multitudes that are admitted to make choice of the persons to be entrusted in the representative."[23] Fourth is the danger, inherent in popular rule, of demagogery: the tendency to choose "the lowest of the people" or those who "satisfy them in all their phrenetic humors."

Nedham's fifth to tenth anti-Leveller arguments amplify his distrust of democracy in 1650. An Agreement of the People or its equivalent would weaken England by replacing statesmen with "busybodies." It would lead to corruption and the buying and selling of public offices. Democratic rotation in office would produce inept and inexperienced leaders. Levelling, which is a consequence of democracy, would be "the only enemy of true generosity and virtue." Moreover, levelling would lead to the curse of economic equality, and this, finally, would culminate in the horror of "absolute community." Thus, Nedham concludes, "those zealous pretenders to liberty and freedom" want to lead the country down "the bloody road to all licentcousness, mischief, mere anarcy and confusion."[24] Nedham used the clichés and shibboleths that the center and right were flinging at the radicals; they had been used for centuries, and they are still current.

The concluding chapter of Nedham's book is affirmative: 'A Discourse of the Excellency of a

Free State above a Kingly Government.' But he begins with an attack on monarchy, again mortaring his argument with a profusion of classical examples and quotations from many authorities, among them Machiavelli. Nedham makes the minor concession "that the kingly are not much less destructive than the leveling popular tyrannies to gallant and worthy men."[25] He moves next to praise of qualified religious toleration, taking a stance somewhat to the right of Cromwell's:

> Prudent toleration of opinions in matter of religion could never be proved yet by any of our Episcoparians and Presbyterians, in all their writings, to be repugnant to the Word; being as far to seek this way as they are to convince us of the sacred necessity of a national uniformity. Several instances there are to show how this Commonwealth hath punished those wild pretenders that profess manifest libertinism and blasphemy, many of whom at this day are in custody. And as long as these ill weeds are rooted out of the garden of the church, the wholesome, tender plants will thrive in beauty and virtue under their several measures and dispensations.[26]

It is in the peroration of The Case of the Commonwealth, however, that Nedham unleashes his professional enthusiasm, becoming almost lyrical in his vision of a properly settled future:

> Therefore if men will not submit and settle but keep the state by their obstinacy under the necessities of war, they must, if they plot or attempt anything against them, expect such proceedings and consequences as attend the sword when it is drawn. But would they close cordially in affection and be resolved once to settle in opposition to all invaders and intruders and let the Commonwealth have leave to take breath a little in the possession of a firm peace, then they would soon find the rivulets of a free state much more pleasing than the troubled ocean of kingly

tyranny; begetting fertility and verdure, as they run along, in all the meadows and reviving those pastures which royalty was wont to drown and swallow. Had they but once tasted the sweets of peace and liberty both together, they would soon be of the opinion of Herodotus and Demosthenes that there is no difference between king and tyrant and become as zealous as the ancient Romans were in defense of their freedom. And though this discourse may sound like that concerning the joys of heaven in the ears of ordinary people, as of blessings afar off, yet since it is in your power to hasten them, why stand ye off and delay? Ye may, if you please, by an unanimous obedience quickly open the fountains of future happiness that justice may run down as a mighty stream in the channel of the laws, and righteousness and peace embrace each other.[27]

But the reiterated message of Nedham's case and Case, in terms of both theory and practise, is his stark translation of Cicero: "All men that would be safe [are advised] to submit unto necessity."[28]

Nedham's combination of hard-nosed expediency and proseletyzing enthusiasm for the Commonwealth was successful enough to call for a second edition of The Case in October. It is almost identical with the first, except for the addition of an eight-page appendix consisting of English translations of passages from Claude Saumaise's Defensio Regia (Nov. 1649) and Thomas Hobbes's De Corpore Politico (March 1650).[29] Both men were, of course, well known Royalists, with international reputations and prestigious audiences. How functional that their most recent publications, as quoted by Nedham, seemed to corroborate his contention that "the power of the sword gives title to government." As he pointedly explained, it was useful to "foil our adversaries with weapons of their own approbation." To underline this, he adds such comments "as Mr. Hobbes saith, There can be no security for life, limbs, and property...

[except] by relinquishing the right of self-protection"; and that the only way to preserve the well-being of England is by "submission to the present power."

Claude Saumaise--Claudius Salmasius--was Milton's adversary, and early in 1951 Milton's "First Defense" answered his Defensio Regia. But the connection between Milton and Nedham is not that tenuous. It is possible that Milton and Nedham met in 1647; in June 1649 Milton was asked to "examine the papers of Pragmaticus and report what he finds in them to the Council [of State]."[30] (Appendix A is a chronology of the friendship between Milton and Nedham.) In May 1650, as we have seen, Nedham was granted a probationary pension of ₤100, plus ₤50 for "service already done": the writing of The Case of the Commonwealth. It was the other part of Nedham's deal, his obligation to edit a pro-government newspaper, in which Milton played a part.

As a leading consultant to the Commonwealth on public relations, Milton probably approved of this journalistic project, and he may have been involved in the selection of Nedham as editor. He was officially connected with the new weekly from Janaury 23, 1651 to January 22, 1652, during which period he served as the special "licenser" of Mercurius Politicus.[31] Even then his role was nominal, since the job of licenser at this time only involved making sure that the journal was periodically entered in the Stationers' Register, along with the names of "the Printers and Authors ...that they may be forth coming if required."[32] Milton did not censor Nedham, though potentially he could have. He may have advised him on what news to stress, assuming that Nedham needed such advice, and he may have helped with the wording of a few editorials in Politicus. But the supposition of Masson, among other of Milton's biographers, that he wrote some of these editorials is wrong.[33] Those attributed to Milton were in fact lifted by the frugal Nedham from his own The Case of the Commonwealth. He and Milton were in the process of becoming friends but, though they shared many ideas, Milton was not the author of even those lead articles which are most Miltonic.

The story of Mercurius Politicus, more than that of Britanicus or Pragmaticus, is revealing about Nedham, the Interregnum, and realpolitik. The weekly press was intermittently a victim of Cromwell's rise to power. In September 1649 a stringent "Act against Unlicensed and Scandalous Bookes and Pamphlets" was put on the statute books, and two years later it was replaced by a similar law.34 The threat of censorship, along with its occasional use, had a stifling effect, and for most of a decade Nedham faced very little journalistic competition. One weekly that lasted slightly more than a year, beginning in October 1649, was edited by Walter Frost, the Secretary of the Council of State. A second, which survived six years, was edited by the official Clerk of the House of Commons or his delegate. A third, which also lasted about six years from December 1649 on, was edited by the Secretary of the Army. Each was therefore docile, limited, and semi-official.35 During 1649 and the first half of 1650 sporadic Royalist journals appeared and reappeared, but in June the editor of the now most durable and scurrilous of them, The Man in the Moon, was arrested.36 For the next year, and only intermittently after that, Nedham until 1659 would have no Royalist mercuries yapping at his heels.

The first number of Mercurius Politicus covered the news from June 6-13, 1650, and it continued to meet this weekly chore and challenge for almost ten years--in a total of approximately 8,000 pages. Indeed, if one adds to this the pages Nedham was responsible for in Britanicus and Pragmaticus, plus those in The Publick Intelligencer, which from late 1655 to early 1660 was the Monday companion to Thursday's Politicus (excluding those pages that repeat Politicus), one arrives at a total of about 12,000 pages.

Five days before the first number of <u>Politicus</u>, and with more than 10,000 pages to come, Nedham submitted to the Council of State a prospectus for his weekly. It was to be published "in defense of the Commonwealth, and for the Information of the People." In order to be "cryed up," it was to be "written in a jocular way," because "Fancy...ever swayes the Scepter in Vulgar Judgement, much more than Reason." The prospectus concludes with the request that the editor be supplied with "the best Ingelligence of State."[37] It was arranged that <u>Politicus</u> be printed by Thomas Newcomb, one of the more successful publishers of pro-Commonwealth books, pamphlets, and official papers;[38] and because of its sixteen-page length, it was to sell for two pennies, twice the cost of the usual weeklies.

Nedham begins the first number by assuring his readers that they are getting their money's worth:

> Why should not the Common-wealth have a Fool, as well as the King had?....But you'll say, I am out of fashion because I make neither Rimes nor Faces, for Fiddlers pay, like the Royal Mercuries. Yet you shall know I have authority enough to create a fashion of my own, and make all the world to follow the humor.

He goes on to claim that though it is "a ticklish time to write Intelligence," he will be honest and fearless.

Because of his official backing, Nedham was kept well informed about what was going on inside the government. He was also able to count on the services of two correspondents in Scotland, one connected with the army, the other with the rudimentary diplomatic service. He had two, sometimes three, knowledgeable men in Paris who kept him au courant on European news, as well as a regular correspondent in The Hague.[39] As a result, the news in <u>Politicus</u> was fuller and more reliable than that in any other Interregnum newspaper.

That Nedham's combination of a jocular style and relatively broad coverage was effective is attested to by the retrospective comments of two Royalists. The first is from a historian who kept a quasi-diary of public events:

> Now appeared in Print, as the weekly Champion of the New Commonwealth, and to bespatter the King with the basest of scurrilous raillery, one Marchamont Nedham, under the name of Politicus, a Jack of all sides, transcendently gifted in opprobrious and treasonable Droll, ...who began his first Diurnal with an Invective against Monarchy and the Presbyterian Scotch Kirk, and ended it with an Hosanna to Oliver Cromwell.[40]

The second is from an attack on Nedham a few months after the Restoration:

> Politicus...flying every week into all parts of the nation, 'tis incredible what influence...[it] had upon numbers of unconsidering persons, who have a strange presumption that all must needs be true that is in Print. This [Nedham] was the great Goliah of the Philistines, the great Champion of the late Usurper, whose Pen was in comparison with others like a Weavers beam: and certainly he that shall peruse these Papers will judge that had the Devil himself (the Father of Lies)...been in this news office, he could not have exceeded him.[41]

Nedham's decade-long career as editor of Politicus earned these implied compliments, and from start to almost-finish his own manner remained assured. In the second number he claimed that both ladies and cavaliers like his weekly because of its "true English" style, though "the Presbyters, they cry out that Politicus is an atheist, because he tosses the Kirk like a football, and jerks their hypocrisy." In July he boasted that his was "the only State-Almanack to tell what the Weather is in the Commonwealth." In

August he managed simultaneously to apologize for and brag about his pre-Commonwealth exploits. He also followed his prospectus by inserting jocular passages. For instance, he often referred to Charles II as "young Tarquin," and he patronized him with a mixture of raillery and mild invective; and the Duke of York consequently becomes, on occasion, "James Tarquin." But the chief asset of <u>Mercurius Politicus</u> was Nedham's sure touch as an editor. Better than any of his colleagues he could condense official reports, as well as letters from his correspondents, and he could support the Commonwealth not only by what news he printed---or omitted, but by adroitly slanting his diction and comments. Yet he usually avoided giving the impression that he was a zealot or a toady.

But with number 16, at the end of September 1650, Nedham's tone became consistently less jocular and flip. Up to then the first page of <u>Politicus</u> had breezily attacked the Scots or Presbyterians or Levellers and praised the Commonwealth--and the editor. From then until October 1651 he began forty-four numbers with serious editorials, none of them written by Milton, all of them lifted by Nedham from his own <u>The Case of the Commonwealth</u>. To look ahead for a moment: after he had finished cannibalizing <u>The Case</u>, Nedham used his next forty-four editorials to constitute a book which was published four years later, <u>The Excellencie Of A Free State</u>. In one instance, one of his "Miltonic" paragraphs appeared first in <u>The Case</u>, then in <u>Politicus</u>, and finally, slightly revised in <u>The Excellencie</u>. Nedham could be expedient in more ways than one. (Appendix B is a chart showing the relationship between the editorials in <u>Politicus</u> and <u>The Case</u> and <u>The Excellencie</u>. It covers <u>Politicus</u> no. 16 to no. 114--Sept. 19, 1650 to Aug. 12, 1652.)

His expediency is also evident in the way he plagiarized from himself. He cut drastically, printing less than one-quarter of <u>The Case</u> as editorials in <u>Politicus</u>. He jettisoned almost all its scholarly apparatus: the marginalia, most Latin and Greek citations, and many of the historical examples. In Philip Knachel's words, Nedham was "clearly...bidding for a larger, less sophisticated audience."[42] He also eliminated large chunks of the book, especially the first chapter where he had argued that all governments "have their Revolutions and fatall Periods," and the chapter on the Levellers. Perhaps the Commonwealth would not be subject to the historical cycle, and the Levellers were ceasing to be a threat.

He also frequently rearranged the order in which both chapters and passages appeared. Sometimes, too, he changed the wording. In The Case, for instance, Charles II is usually "the prince," in Politicus "the young pretender" or "the young Scot." On a few occasions Nedham expanded sentences from The Case to make their impact more specific: for instance, in reference to Charles I's execution, Nedham adds "(as he deserved)." Possibly at Milton's suggestion, he either dropped quotations from Machiavelli or referred to him disparagingly: e.g., in The Case "Machiavelli adviseth," in Politicus "....good advice (though given by Machiavelli.)"[43]

The most significant differences between The Case and Politicus occur on those occasions when Nedham did not take his editorials from the book. And the most striking example is from no. 66, September 4-11, 1651, immediately after the Battle of Worcester. Masson quotes it in full, and discusses it as a striking example of Milton's influence on Nedham; and H. Sylvia Anthony uses it as part of her similar evidence. Also, it shows how much more prone Nedham was to attribute political and military successes to divine rather than to secular causes in Politicus than in The Case. Because this lengthy lead article is a fine example of Nedham's resonant "Miltonic" style, as well as of his ability to invoke God to justify his own political stance in the manner of many of the Independents, it is reprinted at the end of Appendix B.

Regardless of Milton's possible influence or of Nedham's Miltonic streak, the most intriguing connection between Nedham and Milton is that numbers 27 to 36 of <u>Mercurius Politicus</u> reprint the Appendix to the second edition of <u>The Case</u>, but usually without indicating that Nedham is quoting Salamaius and Hobbes. The prominent Milton scholar, J. Milton French, is indignant:

> Thus it appears that for practically two months, under Milton's very nose and while he was licensing the paper personally, Nedham was calmly using as editorials in support of the Grand Old Cause excerpts from Hobbes and from Milton's great antagonist Salmasius. While Milton was losing his eyesight forever from the strain of answering Salmasius the Great, his own paper was feeding Salmasian doctrine to his own public.[44]

I am sure that French is wrong. Milton and Nedham each had a sense of humor, and they remained friends into the 1660's. My conjecture is that Milton must have been amused at this tricky device of Nedham's. I am equally certain that Salmasius was not amused.

The cumulative effect of these forty-four editorials almost certainly helped to gain public support for the Commonwealth--and Nedham was justly earning his double stipend. Moreover, <u>Politicus</u> continued its professional ways. Its coverage of the war with the Scots, culminating in the Battle of Dunbar in 1650, was reliable and often dramatic, as were its accounts of renewed fighting in the spring and summer of 1651. Charles II was temporarily no longer a young fool but a potentially powerful traitor. Nedham, as an insider, was also in a good position to anticipate events. Thus, for instance, early in 1651 he ran several anti-Dutch stories which were prophetic of Anglo-Dutch hostilities in 1652. Finally, Nedham increased his income by printing a growing number of advertisements, mainly for new books, in <u>Politicus</u>.

In October 1651 the editorials extracted from The Case came to an end and, without an intermission, a new series began, which lasted until August 1652. Nedham here seemed to reverse his method of self-plagiarism. These editorials were reprinted in 1656 in an unsigned book, The Excellencie Of A Free State, the title echoing that of the last chapter in The Case. Why did Nedham not acknowledge his authorship, which was obvious to his contemporaries, and why did he delay publication for four years? The answer is mixed.

The final four pages (242-246) of The Excellencie, consisting mainly of long quotations from an Independent sermon preached on November 5, 1651, appeared in Mercurius Politicus, number 74, the following day. Pages 23-242 were serialized, with a few interruptions, during the next nine months, though bits and pieces of the book had been printed earlier, in February and September. Only sections of its first twenty-two pages, which are introductory, were written or modified in 1656. (Again, see Appendix B for a detailed breakdown of the relationship between the book and the journal.)

H. Sylvia Anthony makes a very convincing case that almost all of The Excellencie Of A Free State was written during the year prior to its serialization in Politicus: that is, between late 1650 and November 1651.[45] Thus Nedham again cannibalized his own work to provide himself with weekly editorials. This time, however, he used almost the entire book and made very few changes. It is therefore more functional to discuss The Excellencie as a single work rather than as a series of lead articles. This discussion, in turn, may explain why Nedham delayed its publication for four years and then did not put his name on the title-page.

The Excellencie Of A Free State is Nedham's most radical tract. It endorses a much greater degree of democracy than any of his other works,

93

and it sometimes anticipates the United States Constitution in its advocacy of rotation in office and separation of powers. (The subtitle includes the phrase "The Right Constitution of a Commonwealth," and the author signs himself "a Well-Wisher to Posterity.") But 1656 was different from 1651. Besides pretending anonymity, Nedham in the Preface gives the impression that <u>The Excellencie</u> is in part an answer to James Howell's <u>Some Sober Inspections made into the Late-long Parliament</u> of 1655, and he includes this qualification:

> I believe none will be offended with the following Discourse, but those that are enemies to publick welfare: let such be offended still: it is not for their sakes that I publish this ensuing Treatise; but for your sakes, that have been noble Patriots, fellow-Souldiers, and Sufferers for the Liberties and Freedoms of your Country.

He does not mention the fact that <u>The Excellencie</u> had been serialized in <u>Politicus</u>.

Back in 1651, after the subjugation of Scotland and Ireland and before the Anglo-Dutch wars, Parliament and army, despite the many tensions between them, were still managing to cooperate. Cromwell seemed to most a benevolent semi-dictator. By 1656 as Lord Protector he seemed less benevolent, more dictatorial. The Puritan Revolution had been stabilized, if not reversed; and the temporary local power of the Major Generals was the highly visible and unpopular symbol and symptom of this conservatism. Yet throughout the 1650's, as in the 1640's, public debate about politics and political theory was generally free and wide-ranging.

One esteemed modern historian of political thought, J.G.A. Pocock, describes <u>The Excellencie</u> as "the first sustained example of republican democracy in classical and Machiavellian terms.... The politics of the Roman republic are presented

from a point of view militantly plebian; Athens--
a rare thing at this period--is preferred over
Sparta; and Venice, usually the paragon of mixed
governments, becomes the archetype of 'standing
Aristocracies'."[46] Throughout, Nedham is indeed
profuse in his citation of historical precedents
to support his concept of a democratic government
based on the people's right to bear arms and on
the rotation in office of both legislators and
magistrates. As in The Case, though his conclusions have shifted almost 180 degrees, his argument is logical, his style varied and forceful.

The Introduction centers on Roman history.
"Not only the name of King, but the thing King
(whether in the hands of one or of many) was
pluck'd up root and branch, before ever the Romans
could attain to a full Establishment in their
Rights and Freedoms."[47] Athens gets a lesser
play, though "It is wonderful to consider how
mightily the Athenians were augmented in a few
years, both in Wealth and Power, after they had
freed themselves from the Tyranny of Pistra-
tus."[48]

Nedham next elaborates on 'The Right Constitution of a Commonwealth.' In approximately sixty
pages he attempts to show that "the end of all
Government being the good & ease of the people,
they best know where the shooe pinches."[49] On
the other hand, "The Interest of Freedom is a Virgin that everyone seeks to deflower; and like a
Virgin, it must be kept from any other Form, or
else (so great is the Lust of mankinde for dominion) there follows a rape upon the first opportun-
ity."[50] To resolve this Hobbesian dilemma
Nedham advocates rotation in office. Authority,
as in Plato's Republic, should be a burden rather
than a benefit. Also, by limiting the length of
time a man can be legislator or a magistrate, a
Commonwealth can secure itself against corruption,
faction, self-seeking. In such a Free State "the
People are ever indued with a more magnanimous,
active, and noble temper of Spirit than under the
Grandeur of any standing power whatsoever. And

this arises from the apprehension which every particular man hath of his own immediate share in the publick Interest, as well as of that security which he possesses in the enjoyment of his private Fortune, free from the reach of any Arbitrary Power."[51] Such a form of government is therefore "most suitable to the Nature and Reason of Mankinde."[52]

If parts of The Excellencie anticipate the United States Constitution, one sentence near the end of this section is strangely prophetic of Watergate and the problem of Nixon's pardon: in a Free State "all powers are accountable for misdeameanors...in regard of the nimble Returns and Periods of the Peoples Election: by which means, he that ere-while was a Governour, being reduced to the condition of a Subject, lies open to the force of the Laws, and may with ease be brought to punishment for his offence; so that after the observation of such a course, others which succeed will become the less daring to offend."[53]

In supporting 'The Right Constitution of a Commonwealth' Nedham attacks the Presbyterians for their intolerance and the Scottish chiefs for their arbitrary local powers; and with another bouquet of classical examples he asserts and reasserts the citizens' right to bear arms and to participate in the law-making process.

Then for approximately another sixty pages he tries to answer 'All Objections Against the Government of the People.' The Excellencie may be Nedham's most radical tract, but he was not a republican and certainly not a Leveller. A Free State can be anti-monarchist and anti-oligarchical without going as far as the Agreement of the People and without endangering private property. Thus he takes a stand against universal manhood sufferage, though he remains deliberately vague on who is eligible to vote:

> As to...a Commonwealth in its settled and composed state, when all men within it are

presumed to be its Friends, questionless, a right to chuse and to be chosen is then to be allowed the people (without distinction) in as great a latitude as may stand with right Reason and Convenience, for managing a matter of so high Consequence as their Supreme Assemblies, wherein somewhat must be left to humane Prudence; and therefore that latitude being to be admitted more or less, according to the Nature, Circumstances, and Necessities of any Nation, is not here to be determined.[54]

The Levellers had proposed excluding from the franchise only those receiving alms, "servants to, and receiving wages from any particular person," and--for seven years--Royalists. Nedham also excludes Royalists, but he is much less inclusive and explicit than the Levellers. Further, he hedges his support of rotation in office by distinguishing between "acts of state" and "secrets of state." His treatment of the latter suggests his approval of some kind of semi-permanent civil service and, by implication, of a Council of State that has continuity of membership.[55] Finally, in answering "all Objections" he makes it clear that he is a respecter of private property and that this version of a Free State is conducive to stability and economic growth.

The next section of The Excellencie becomes slightly more theoretical as it attempts to show that 'The Original of all just Power is in the People.' Yet Nedham basically emphasizes the negative: "When the mystery of Tyranny is undress't, and stript of all its gaudy robes, and gay Appearances, it may be hiss't out of the Civill part of mankind, into the company of the more barbrous and brutish Nations."[56] By castigating various kinds of "Tyranny" Nedham edges toward the justification of democracy.

He edges a little closer in the next, and longest, section of The Excellencie: 'Errours of Government, And Rules of Policy.' Throughout the book, but especially in this chapter, the reader is aware of the tension between Nedham's belief in some kind of popular government and his fear of instability and anarchy, though this tension was much less evident in the individual editorials when they came out in <u>Politicus</u>.

He begins by stating his Erastian belief that the state is superior to the church. But to avoid tyranny the state must allow wide religious toleration; and with many anti-clerical touches he warns against Catholic, Prelatical, and Presbyterian "Clergy-Interest." He is also a constitutionalist, and he goes on to say that the people must "keep steadily" to the rules of a Free State:

> For they should not only know what Freedom is, and have it represented in all its lively and lovely Features, that they may grow zealous and jealous over it; but, that it may be a Zeal according to knowledge and good purpose: it is without all question, most necessary, that they be made acquainted, and thoroughly instructed in the Measures and Rules of its preservations, against the Adulterous Wiles and Rapes of any projecting Sophisters that may arise hereafter.[57]

After this lyrical passage Nedham itemizes nine ways that have worked in the past to keep the people properly involved and wary. In very abbreviated form they are:

1) "To abjure a toleration of Kings and Kingly Government."

2) "Not to suffer particular Persons to Grandise or greaten themselves."

3) "Not to permit a Continuation of Command and Authority in the hands of particular persons or families."

4) Not to allow two members of one family to hold power at the same time.

5) To uphold "the Majesty and Authority" of the "Supream Assemblies" which they elect.

6) "To see that the people be continually trained up in the Exercise of Arms, and the Militia lodged onely in the Peoples hands.... [because] The Sword and Soveraignity ever walk hand in hand together."

7) To make sure that "children... [are] educated and instructed in the Principles of Freedom."

8) To remember that the people must "observe moderation" in their use of liberty; that they should not over-react against temporary flaws; that they should avoid faction and calumny; and that they should be alert to merit and suspicious of flattery.

9) To alert the people that violation of their trust is treason.

Nedham then comes back to 'Errours of Government, And Rules of Policy.' His threefold concluding message is that history has cumulatively shown the dangers of tyranny and "Reasons of State," that rotation in office and the separation of "the Legislative and Executive Powers of a State" are essential to Freedom, and that the people must, at this crucial moment in English history, avoid faction and impatience. Surprisingly, ten of these final forty pages are devoted to refuting Machiavelli's The Prince on both pragmatic and moral grounds, culminating in Nedham's own conclusion, which is in context both pragmatic and moral:

> The onely way to preserve liberty in the hands of a people, that have gained it by the Sword, is to put it in the peoples hands, that is, into the hands of such, as by a contribution of their purses, strengths, and counsells, have all along asserted it, without the least strain of corruption, staggering, or

apostacie; for in this case, these are only to be reckoned the people.[58]

Nedham's final definition in The Excellencie Of A Free State of who deserves the franchise corresponds to Milton's definition of who deserves to be free.

What, then, was the mixture of rashness and timidity in Nedham's decision to publish The Excellencie in 1656? First, the leftist impact of the book was almost certainly greater than that of the forty-four separate editorials in 1651-52.[59] Second, Nedham's timing of the publication was risky. He had entered the book in the Stationers' Register in November 1655. On June 26, 1656 Cromwell consented to the calling of a new Parliament and passed the word that he would not interfere in the elections. Three days later The Excellencie came out. Probably the moment seemed propitious to Nedham, and by this time he must have felt that Cromwell owed him a debt for many services rendered. Third, Nedham did indulge in some hedging. He qualified a few of the more radical statements that had appeared in Politicus and omitted a few others. Also, he eliminated the final editorial in the series, a vigorous plea for disestablishment of the church. A state-supported church, Nedham had written, is in "the interest, not of Christ but the clergy."[60] Nedham was being prudent to omit this. Cromwell was a dictator who believed in some civil liberties and in a high level of religious toleration, but he was not prepared to see the church totally cast loose from state support. Despite these changes, Nedham was sticking his neck out by publishing The Excellencie, though Cromwell did not chop off his head. Au contraire.

That Nedham was relatively daring and Cromwell relatively tolerant is indicated by the revival of the book in the late eighteenth century. It was republished in London in 1767, and reissued, with an Amsterdam imprint, in 1774.[61] The radical Thomas Hollis sent a copy of The

Excellencie to America, where it was carefully read by John Adams in the 1780's, and later by John Quincy Adams.62 In 1790 it was published in Paris, in a French translation. The lengthy Preface includes praise for Nedham as a man who nourished "le droit inaliénable de l'homme á la liberté," and who helped to pave the way for the "triomphe de l'homme sur la tyrannie et sur le despotisme."

Predictably Nedham soon reneged. His last editorial had appeared in Mercurius Politicus in the summer of 1652. In March 1657 he printed four semi-facetious editorials, the only additional ones he ever wrote.63 Their purpose was to prepare the public for the restoration of monarchy, with Cromwell as king. In the form of letters from Utopia, they invoke Sir Thomas More. More, Nedham says, wrote in a style "betwixt jest and earnest," but when "falling from his principle by being once in his days in earnest," he got himself beheaded for supporting the Pope, thus proving it is wrong to be too serious "amongst the great politicians of this captious world." Nedham admires More, but he pointedly ridicules James Harrington and his republican colleagues. This ridicule italicizes Nedham's cop-out, for it is probable that Harrington directly or indirectly encouraged him to publish The Excellencie Of A Free State. Certainly it shares many ideas with Harrington's Oceana, also published in 1656. (A gloating Royalist pamphlet in March 1660, The Character of the Rump, claimed that Nedham "was one of the spokes in Harrington's Rota, till he was turned out for cracking."64 Doubtless this refers to the winter of 1659-60, for Harrington's society for the discussion of constitutional schemes lasted only from November to February. Presumably Nedham and Harrington remained at least on speaking terms. Yet the republican spoke really cracked in 1657, despite Nedham's later sporadic efforts at self-repair.)

Collectively, these four editorials satirize all political theorists, and they conclude that any de facto authority should be obeyed. Nedham is here at his most expedient, his most cynical. He asserts that in seven years of political experimentation the Utopians had proved their madness: believing in principles of natural right and freedom, they had lost sight of the fact that government is "an art or artifice...occasioned by necessity."

> For the rulers and reasons of government cannot be always the same, it depending upon future contingents, and therefore must be alterable according to the variety of emergent circumstances and accidents;...and so a free state may be no less, and many times much more, in that which men call monarchy, than in any other form....Men are as free every jot under a right principality as under a popular form.

In the final "letter from Utopia" Nedham concludes that "'tis neither dishonour nor scandal...after all other experiments made in vain, where the ends of government cannot otherwise be conserved, to revert upon the old bottom and foundation." The old bottom was of course a monarchy. The former editor of <u>Mercurius Pragmaticus</u> was now hailing King Oliver with respect, not derision.

Among the political theorists whom Nedham mocked in these four editorials was the Marchamont Nedham who in the early 1650's had written <u>The Case of the Commonwealth</u> and <u>The Excellencie Of A Free State</u>: "that wondrous wise Republican called Mercurius Politicus (who served up the Politicks in Sippets)." But as editor of <u>Mercurius Politicus</u> he remained consistently assured and professional until the end of the decade, and he never in its pages indulged in self-mockery.

Back in the winter of 1650-51 Milton had presumably been amused by Nedham's use of those monarchists, Salmasius and Hobbes, in his editorials taken from <u>The Case</u>. Milton's own reply to Salmasuis, <u>Defensio pro Populo Anglicano</u>, came out in February 1651. Nedham's skill as a journalist is shown in his reporting of this work. In January <u>Politicus</u> printed two stories to the effect that anti-monarchists on the Continent were worried that Salmasius had not yet been refuted. Early in February Nedham's correspondent in The Hague reported that he was "thankfully glad of the promise <u>Politicus</u> gives us of <u>Salmasius</u> answer, which we greedily expect." In March the same correspondent wrote that "Salmasius is not like to live to make any Reply to <u>Milton's</u> book, which here is very much applauded. It seems he is very ill in Sweden." In a letter from Amsterdam dated March 28 the readers of <u>Politicus</u> were informed that:

> <u>Miltoni Defensionem pro Populo Anglicano</u>, I got here lately and perused it with much satisfaction: Tomorrow, God willing, I send it to a Counsellor of the Elector of Brandenburg. The author (it seems) is a man of singular parts, acuteness and solidity. Some perhaps may finde fault with the personall jerks therein; but the least review of <u>Salmasius</u> will show what tuned the <u>Eccho</u> to such a <u>Key</u>. I am sure if he lives yet, he will finde worke enough, and tough, to disentangle himself handsomly in the main.

In July Nedham happily reported that the Catholics had publickly burnt Milton's book in Toulouse and Paris. Then for several months he printed derogatory stories about Salmasius's discomfiture and his consequent illnesses and wanderings. For instance, Salmasius left Sweden because Milton "laid him open so notoriously" that the Queen would not long give refuge to "so pernitious a Parasite and Promoter of Tyranny." The story petered out by November. Thereafter Milton's name appeared in <u>Politicus</u> very infrequently, though between 1654 and 1660 six of his works, starting with <u>Defensio Secunda</u> and ending with <u>The Ready and Easy Way</u>, were advertised in the newspaper.[65]

Nedham was professionally involved with another well-known English author, John Selden. In November 1652 <u>Of the Dominion, Or Ownership of</u>

the Sea was published by "special Command." Originally written in Latin by Selden in 1635, it could now be useful as propaganda against the Dutch. Nedham was asked to translate it and to add a few up-to-date "Evidences and Discourses." In a Dedicatory Epistle to Parliament, after praising Selden, he attacks the Dutch and reaffirms England's right to control the seas--and he of course eliminates the original dedication to the King. He urges Parliament to be militant against the enemy, for among their many crimes the most heinous is their "invasion of English seas." Then come the 459 pages of his translation, followed by his assemblage of "Additional Evidences...Collected Out of certain publick Papers, relating to the Reigns of K. James, and K. Charles."[66] The book ends with a piece written earlier, not by Nedham, entitled "The inestimable Riches and Commodities of the British Seas."[67] Du-Gard, perhaps London's most prestigious publisher, did a fine job of printing and binding this massive accolade to British imperialism. Nedham was duly rewarded: in February 1653 the Council of State ordered that he be paid an extra ₤10 for his translation.[68]

During all these years Nedham continued to receive his annual ₤100 as editor of *Mercurius Politicus*. Sometimes he was paid in a lump sum, sometimes in two installments, sometimes quarterly.[69] But he did get paid and he did earn his keep. *Mercurius Politicus* for almost ten years remained England's largest-selling and most influential weekly.[70] After its sixteenth number Nedham used the "jocular" tone less frequently, and his paper became generally impersonal. It was set up in type each day, as the news came in. If the news piled upon on Wednesday, the day before publication, the printer used increasingly smaller type on the last page or two. Nedham's correspondents continued to be capable, and he himself stayed close to the centers of power in London. Starting late in 1652 or early in 1653 John Thurloe, the head of the Cromwellian equivalent of the FBI and CIA, succeeded Milton as the official licenser of Politicus.[71] With his occasional guidance Nedham was enabled to loft trial balloons, spread certain rumors, and suppress a few dangerous stories.[72] Finally, Nedham almost certainly had editorial and office-boy help when he needed it.

Nedham prospered. The weekly circulation of Politicus was probably a little more than 1,000, higher when big news was breaking. At two pence a copy, the editor and the printer made, between them, a penny a copy. Because of Nedham's position and prominance, he probably got more than half of that profit. The charge for advertisements was six pence or a shilling. Book advertisements were the staple, and one issue of Politicus carried ninteen, though by 1655 seven or eight had become the average. Closely behind them came advertisements for medicines.[73]

Nedham edited the news well and he could be expert in condensing it. His coverage of the Anglo-Dutch naval wars, for instance, was usually terse and graphic, and he had a feel for drama and suspense. In reporting domestic news he was generally a subtle rather than a blatant propagandist, and much of the overseas news in Politicus was slightly slanted so that it was favorable to the Commonwealth and flattering to English chauvinism. Nedham enjoyed deriding the Scots and their Kirk, but again he usually combined this with some sort of appeal to English pride. For most of the decade he was effective in belittling Charles II and the exiled court:

> the King and his family are said to be great Readers and Admirers of Playbooks and Romances; but truly that is little honour to them, so the worst part of the scene is that they themselves are become not onely actors, but real Tragedies and Romances to the World.[74]

Thus they "linger at St. Germans building Castles in the air," in an atmosphere of intrigue, debauchery, and poverty.

In the autumn of 1654 Parliament ordered that no news of its activities be printed without a license from its Clerk, and <u>Mercurius Politicus</u> was the only weekly so honored.[75] Nedham's journalistic clout, despite the fact that other weeklies did not adhere to this order, was further increased. In the middle of the decade, via the reports of a member of the English entourage in Sweden, the reader of <u>Politicus</u>, then as now, could follow the intricacies and savor the tensions of diplomatic bargaining; and the paper's accounts of the massacre of the Piedmontese Protestants are still bloodcurdling. Occasionally Nedham ran stories from exotic places like China and Turkey, and in the summer of 1654 he reported the arrival of a group of Brazilian Jews in Holland.[76] His stories about the Royalists in exile continued to make Charles and his coterie seem feeble and inept, sometimes comic, never dangerous.

<u>Mercurius Politicus</u> was also effective in its handling of local news. Its few crime stories are properly gory. Occasionally it printed what can be called anecdotes, one of which has all the elements of a Saki short story in which a man values a valet more than he does his wife: the cook of a Highland laird was captured, and the laird was willing to go to great lengths to get him released.[77] Surprisingly modern is the account of a strike in Newcastle. An embryonic labor movement did exist in Interregnum England. In London the Levellers had agitated for higher wages and better working conditions, the Diggers had tried to collectivize a few farmers, scattered miners' strikes had occurred in the west, and there had been sporadic rumblings among the dockworkers.

> We have had a great stop of Trade by our Keelmens pretence of too small wages from their masters; they all as one man stood together, and would neither worke themselves, nor suffer others, though our Mayor used all possible means to satisfie them; whereupon

he made a Proclamation, but all was to no purpose. And now though a Company of foot and a Troop of Horse be drawn into Town, yet they continue in their obstinacie, notwithstanding that some of their Leading men have been apprehended. The Justices intend to meet and try if they can compose the business.[78]

Presumably the strike was easily broken, for the Keel-men did not reappear in the pages of Politicus. Other bits from the paper seem equally modern: an advertisement for a medicine called "The Duchess of Kent's Powder," several pseudo-scientific stories about a mechanical ship being built in Rotterdam--which turned out to be a hoax, and a few commercial schemes which still sound enticing.[79]

In the summer of 1655 Cromwell ordered that the laws controlling the press be implemented, and three newly apppointed commissioners, among them the Lieutenant of the Tower, went to work. By October these men, backed by the army, had done their job. Nedham now had a monopoly on printing the weekly news, a monopoly which he retained until the spring of 1659. Nedham did not gloat over the extinction of his competition, but he did raise his charge for an advertisement to half a crown.[80] From 1655 to 1659, according to a contemporary source, Nedham's annual income from journalism exceeded ₤500.[81] Milton's top official salary was ₤288, 18s. 6d.[82]

At the end of 1653 Cromwell had become "Lord Protector of the Commonwealth of England." As his power increased and his iron hand grew more evident than his velvet glove, the resistance to him from the left mounted. The Royalists had been routed, and from mid-1655 to the end of 1656 eleven Major Generals imposed law and order on the English countryside. The government secret service under Thurloe was efficient, the army was united behind Cromwell, and he was generally popular--except among the more militant supporters of the Good Old Cause. They had to be watched, and

Cromwell and Thurloe requisitioned Nedham, among others, to watch them. For four years England's richest and most successful journalist became a part-time spy for the government.[83]

His first job in this capacity occurred at the very end of 1653, when he gave a lengthy straightforward report to the Council of State on a meeting of Fifth Monarchists he attended at Blackfriars. The meeting opened with a Scripture lesson, but promptly moved to politics. Vavasour Powell appealed to God to find out whether it was His will that Cromwell should rule over England. For in war Cromwell "was the graciousest of and most gallant man...but when he came home to government, the worst." Christopher Feake, the other leader of the meeting, described the protector as "the most dissembling and perjured villain in the world."[84]

As a result of Nedham's report Feake was imprisoned for four days. Powell was brought before the Council of State but released. Both men continued to attack the government and were briefly jailed. Again they did not remain quiet.[85] The Fifth Monarchist leaders combined religious mysticism with hard-headed radicalism, and they were fiery and effective speakers who could not be silenced by mild sentences. Nedham's first report as a spy was cool, but it dealt with a hot problem.

In February 1654 he reported on another Fifth Monarchist meeting. Again his report was cool, even at time witty, but the implications of his recommendations are neither:

> Marchamont Nedham to the Protector. Wishing to know how the pulse beats at Allhallows, I went there last night. It was a dull assembly without Feake and Simpson, for they were the men that carried it on with heat. [They were then in jail.] Highland, John Spencer, and Mr. Jessey, who now conduct it, are no Boanerges, as you know. But the congregation

is crowded, the humours boiling, and as much scum comes off as ever, but more warily. Highland preached on the 8 beatitudes, but chiefly enlarged on the 2 last, relating to persecution, to which they now fit all their discourses. He magnified the happiness of the 2 sufferers now in prison, prayed for them, and prophesied their deliverance, and the confusion of all enemies, quoted the Apocalypse, and told the people the time was at hand when they should feed on the flesh of kings and great men.

John Spence then spoke from Isaiah, c. 43, v. 1-4, to the like effect, but very cautiously. He also prayed for that servant of God now to be confined, which raised a murmur of inquiry. Jessey spoke softly, and I could not hear him.

There is reason for the total dissolution of that meeting, as you have proceeded against the leaders, and a digest of the paper I have given in, with comments upon them, should be printed at the same time.

This meeting much diminishes your reputation among foreigners, who expect changes, because they are proclaimed from the pulpit, and great things are made of it, though it is but a confluence of silly wretches.

There is a twofold design about the prophetess Hannah [Trapnel], who played her part lately at Whitehall at the ordinary; one to print her discourses and hymns, which are desperate against your person, family, children, friends, and the government; the other to send her all over England, to proclaim them <u>viva voce</u>.[86] She is much visited, and does a world of mischief in London, and would do in the country. The vulgar dote on vain prophecies. I saw hers in the hands of a man who was in the room when she uttered them day by day in her trance, as they call it. He promised to lend me them; if he does, I will show you them. they would make 14 or 15 sheets in print.[87]

Nedham turned in similar reports in April and May 1655, and between 1653 and 1657 he undoubtedly delivered others, especially to Thurloe, of which no record remains.[88] In the spring of 1657 a government official noted that "Nedham, our news writer, being last night in Dr. Goodwin's chamber at Whitehall, the Protector [the following day] asked him the news. He told him that **vox populi** said Mr. Nye should be Archbishop of Canterbury, and Dr. Owen of York."[89] It was a risky joke: if Cromwell had the power and trappings of a monarch, why should not two of the leading Independent ministers become archbishops; or the reverse--no bishop, no king. If Cromwell laughed, it was one of the few times he was able to take the chronic problem of church government unsolemnly. The anecdote also suggests that Nedham was intimate enough with Cromwell to tease him.

In addition to taking the pulse of the left-wing opposition for Thurloe and the Protector, Dr. Nedham supplemented his visit to Goodwin with a 150-page signed attack on the minister, published in July. <u>The Great Accuser Cast Down; Or, A Publick Trial of Mr. John Goodwin...At the Bar of Religion & Right Reason</u> indirectly narrates how a revolution loses momentum, halts, then reverses itself, and how, in the process, former allies become enemies, former enemies become allies. In April 1653 Cromwell had dissolved what was left of the Long Parliament, the Rump. In July he summoned an "assembly" of 140 men selected by the army leaders from nominees of the Independent congregations: the Barebones Parliament, named after one of its members. It split between radicals and conservatives, and in December the latter group manipulated its dissolution. A few high army officers then produced a new constitution, the Instrument of Government, under which Cromwell became Lord Protector. A new Parliament was convened in September 1654, but when it began to tamper with the Instrument of Government Cromwell dissolved it. He next tried ruling with the Major Generals, but in September 1656 a new

Parliament was summoned, mainly to finance England's foreign wars and adventures. Early in 1657, after much debate, Parliament produced the Humble Petition and Advice. Cromwell was offered the crown, and a Parliament of two Houses was reestablished. After much soul-searching, Cromwell refused the title of King, but despite the opposition of the army, he accepted most of the rest of the Humble Petition. This was the background to <u>The Great Accuser Cast Down</u>. These were also the events which Nedham judiciously covered as editor of <u>Mercurius Politicus</u>.

Of course in hindsight, and possibly for Nedham, these events foretold the immediate future. Parliament met in Janaury 1658, with many hitherto excluded members admitted after they had taken an oath to be loyal to the Protector. Many of them, however, on both left and right, opposed the constitution under which they convened, and in February Cromwell dissolved this Parliament. Cromwell was almost sixty, and for the past two decades his life had been strained and strenuous. That he would not live much longer was probable. He died in September and was succeeded by his eldest son Richard, whom he had been empowered to name by the Humble Petition. During this period Nedham flourished. as is corroborated by his correspondence with a Dorset squire, John Fitzjames. A moderate, Fitzjames had been suspicious of the Commonwealth and angered by the Major Generals, but in the spring of 1658 he was enjoying both the stability of the Protectorate and fox-hunting with Richard Cromwell. Apparently Nedham agreed with him that the present government had managed "to settle and consolidate...all considerable parties."[90]

Fitzjames was too optimistic. During these five years of constitutional maneuverings, and the bitter and widespread debates they engendered, the issue of government support of the church--of disestablishement and tithes--clearly separated radical and conservative. The Cromwellian church settlement of 1654 was tolerant, but it maintained some governmental financing of the clergy, and it set up a system of local "Triers" to eliminate "scandalous ministers."

John Goodwin was by no means scandalous. He was a friend of Milton's, who may have occasionally attended his Coleman Street church. In June 1660 he, with Milton, was ordered into custody. Both men went into hiding, and later were granted partial indemnity. Like Milton, Goodwin had long been an Independent. He too attacked the Presbyterians, rated much space in Edwards' Gangraena, and favored the King's execution. Both men were Arminians and supporters of wide religious toleration, though Goodwin was to the left of Milton in his ardor for republicanism.[91]

In May 1657, in The Triers Tried, Goodwin attacked the Cromwellian church arrangements, despite the fact that most of the Triers were fellow Independents. Nedham was immediately commissioned to answer him. In the words of Goodwin's nineteenth-century biographer, Nedham "was bankrupt in character; so that, having nothing to lose, he was a fit person to undertake the defense of any cause."[92]

Nedham began his defense of the Cromwellian cause with a eulogistic dedication to the Protector, but its opening sentence sets the mocking tone of much of his attack on Goodwin:

> It is a Custom in all Countries, when any man hath taken a strange creature, immediately to present it to the Prince: Whereupon, I having taken one of the strangest that (I think) any part of your Highness Dominion hath these many years produced, do with all submissiveness make bold to present him bound hand and foot with his own Cords (as I ought to bring him) to your Highness.

The ensuing 'To the Reader' is one of the more sustained and scathing sneers in Interregnum sub-literature. First, the patronizing touch:

> I must profess in dealing with his [Goodwin's] arguments, I was possessed with an equal temperature of indignation and pity; pity to see him, an ancient minister of the Gospel, and one who a good while ago had a reputation of being conscientious, so plainly to prevaricate in point of conscience, to the reviling of Authority and abuse of his Brethren, even while he is, as it were, sounding the trumpet to his own final dissolution....On the other side, my indignation arose to observe that a man whose writings show him to be a scholar, should yet write so unlike a scholar as he hath done...he loseth himself, and leads the unwary reader quite out of the road of common sense and honesty.

Then, after a sarcastic summary of Goodwin's life and writings, comes the concluding twist of the polemical knife:

> A wise man he is without question, and stronger than a whole city, because having first conquered or corrupted all the world with the help of a printing press, the completest conquest of all is this last, whereby he hath confuted himself. So I commit him to the press, in part of punishment, that he may know himself mortal, and from thence to the winding-sheet, earth to earth, ashes to ashes: peace to all the church: farewell, J.G.

This premature obituary is followed by 132 pages of detailed refutation of Goodwin's arguments. Nedham may have been assisted in this chore by Philip Nye, his facetious candidate for Archbishop of Canterbury and at that time Cromwell's favorite Independent minister.[93] Though most of this refutation is quibbling and solemn, Nedham does insert a few light touches, such as when he praises Goodwin's "great ingenuity to forbear particulars."[94] Throughout he criticises Goodwin's lack of respect for Authority, for the State. Christ, unlike Goodwin, did not advocate rules to exclude the Magistrate from using "his wisdom and endeavours" to spread the Gospel. Nedham also accuses Goodwin of being too Arminian and, along with Roger Williams, of preaching too inclusive a form of religious toleration.[95]

Nedham was incisively answered by Goodwin, who indulged in his own brand of name-calling, and even more vigorously by a certain D.F., "a Person of Quality."[96] Goodwin was merely "reprimanded" by the Council of State, and was not brought to trial or punished. This explains why an alleged tract by Nedham, The Trial of Mr. John Goodwin, was almost certainly never written, and why it is listed in Donald Wing's A Gallery of Ghosts.[97]

Nedham's main job of course remained the editing of Mercurius Politicus. Beginning in the autumn of 1655 he had a monopoly of the weekly press, and he promptly took advantage of this. Besides raising his charges for advertisements, he now brought out his paper in two sixteen-page editions: Politicus on Thursdays, and The Publick Intelligencer on Mondays. Both were comparatively well printed and both were regularly entered in the Stationers' Register. Nedham frequently touched base with Thurloe, who in addition to his other duties was now Cromwell's Postmaster General, Secretary of State, and Supervisor of the Press.[98] To Nedham's credit, he apparently declined Thurloe's or some other high official's suggestion that he become one of a small group for "licensing of books."[99]

Nedham was energetic but not wasteful. From start to finish the overlap between Politicus and The Publick Intelligencer was considerable. Most of the domestic news, almost half of the foreign news, and more than half of the advertisements were reprinted verbatim. Further, he generally handled the foreign news by printing half of his Continental correspondents' reports on Thursdays, the other half on Mondays. Again his income rose, and he augmented it for a few months by arranging to have Politicus reprinted in Edinburgh.[100]

Adeptly he supported the government in both weeklies, and he was trenchant in his attacks on its opponents, whether Fifth Monarchists, Quakers, Levellers, Presbyterians, or Royalists. For instance, when Edward Sexby, a former Leveller who was arrested for plotting to assassinate Cromwell, died in jail, Nedham stressed his quasi-insanity and his confession and repentance, then went on to give a clinical description of Sexby's final illness--probably to forestall any rumors that he had been murdered.[101] In contrast to his elaborate treatment of Sexby's death, Nedham handled other ticklish stories by being terse and cryptic. The arrest of the intransigent republican Sir Henry Vane, the dissolution of Parliament, the recall of the Rump, each received only a few lines.[102] When Parliament was in session the two weeklies usually printed only bare reports, describing legislation that had been enacted but avoiding comment on debates. Nedham, however, could take shorthand, and on a few occasions his coverage of Westminster was full and graphic--and strongly pro-Protectorate.[103]

Consistently he devoted more than half his space to foreign news. Despite the fact that <u>Politicus</u> and the <u>Intelligencer</u> had no competition, their reporting of Continental news was generally extensive, coherent, and--considering the vicissitudes of transmission--reliable. Nedham cut down on the number of stories about Charles II, and during the later 1650's those he printed contained more vitriol and less tolerant amusement than they had at the start of the decade. As the Restoration grew more imminent, he further reduced the space allotted to the man whose exile was nearing an end.

Nedham was still competent in filling any leftover space with noncontroversial local and crime stories and sporadic somewhat tongue-in-cheek accounts of miracles, apparitions, and prodigies. Among the more interesting items for the modern reader are his coverage of the controversial negotiations between Cromwell and Menasseh ben Israel for the readmission of Jews to England, and of the persecution of a deluded messiah, James Nayler, whose cruel punishment the Protector tried to mitigate; the noncontroversial accounts of the departure, after several months in London, of the "Ambassador from the King of Florida," and of the "Opera" at Drury Lane.[104] One story, from Breslau, reads like the archetype of Byron's 'Mazeppa'; another, from Surat, suggests Kipling in its plea that the English colonize and civilize India.[105]

In the autumn of 1657 Nedham covered Lilburne's funeral in one page, Cromwell's a year later in three.[106] Yet his panegyric on Cromwell is a restrained and in many ways honest summary. After referring to "the many strange revolutions of Providence, high contradictions, and wicked conspiracies" which Cromwell had faced, Nedham concludes:

> ...His first undertakings for the Publick Interest, his working things all along, as it were out of the Rocks, his founding a Military Discipline in these Nations such as is not to be found in any example of preceding times... his Wisdom and Piety in things divine, his Prudence in management of the Civil Affairs, and conduct of the Military, and admirable Successes in all made him a Prince indeed among the people of God....[107]

Nedham did not write an elegy on Cromwell, but this prose epitaph is, I think, as valid and as moving as Marvell's lengthy, personal and generally traditional tribute, and certainly more valid and moving than Dryden's cool and chauvinistic outpouring in verse.

Book advertisements remained Nedham's staple, but more interesting are paid notices, such as poignant requests for information about a lost mute or two abandoned infants or some runaway girls.[108] A few are tantalizing: who stole, or where is, a painting by Van Dyke? Or, has anyone seen a man "who went from his keeper?"[109] One notice about two escaped convicts is almost Dickensian:

> ...Walter Frick, a little fellow aged about 22 years, flaxen haired, whitely faced, in a gray cloth sute trimmed with black Ribbon, and a large gray hat edged on the brim with a silk and silver edgeing; and John Smith, a middle sized man with fair hair, a sad coloured Searge sute, with two rows of black hair buttons down the breeches, a stuffe sad coloured large coat with sleeves, a large pair of boots, and a sad gray hat, with a freckled face and a thin sharp nose...[110]

Some of these ads sound extremely modern: a plug for a treatise on how to attain "Peace...of Minde"; the first advertisements for tea and beer; a notice about a new kind of fire extinguisher, another about an improved bed for the sick; an announcement from a man that he would not be responsible for his wife's future debts.[111] Sometimes they employed the hard sell, particularly some of the longer notices about new books and a three-and-a-half-page promotion of stock in the East India Company.[112] On a few occasions an advertisement might be unintentionally humorous, like this announcement from a seventeenth-century Colonel Blimp:

> These are to advertise those persons who have printed the Catlogue of the Names of the Members of the present Parliament that they ought to correct it in severall places, and particularly in Suffolk, where for the County they have printed Thomas Barnardiston Esq, instead of Sir Thomas Barnardiston Knight.[113]

Probably Nedham did not solicit these ads; they came to him.

But three months after Sir Thomas had paid Nedham a shilling for running his snobbish--and symptomatic--complaint, Nedham in May 1659 was outsted from his editorship. His job was temporarily given to John Canne, a Baptist minister who ten years earlier had been a vociferous opponent of the Levellers. For three months Nedham was on the outside looking in--and on. But why now this game of musical chairs?

Between Cromwell's death and the return of Charles the political scene shifted rapidly and confusedly for both scene-setters and onlookers. The leaders of the army, without Cromwell's prestige and firm hand, quickly proved themselves inept and short-sighted. The Republicans were rigid and equally short-sighted. The Presbyterians were equally inept but lucky. Monk, in Scotland, coolly waited, then acted--or, rather, reacted. Charles II, on the Continent, also waited, if not coolly, at least not impetuously. During these twenty months the Restoration steadily became a certainty, though amid the murk of controversy and maneuvering many at first did not see this, or they shut their eyes to the facts of political life. Nedham, like Milton, was one of a small minority who both foresaw the Restoration and fought against it.

Richard Cromwell was a country squire, not a leader of men. Parliament met in January 1659 and officially recognized him as Protector. But the Republicans in Parliament quickly allied themselves with the more radical leaders of the army, and in April they forced Richard to dissolve Parliament. In May the generals restored the remnant of the Rump, Richard returned to rural fox-hunting, and Nedham was fired. Relations between army and Parliament rapidly worsened, and in October the generals dissolved this Parliament. Monk, with his disciplined--and paid--troops, began to march south. Lambert's opposing army, mainly because of lack of pay, evaporated. Monk crossed the border into England, and in December the generals recalled the Rump. On February 3, 1660 Monk entered London. Supported by the leading conservative forces there, as well as by the street crowds, he put pressure on Parliament to readmit those members purged in 1648. In March Parliament fulfilled its pledge to him and his cohorts by dissolving themselves, having provided for new elections. On April 25 the resultant Parliament convened, dominated by a heavy Royalist-Presbyterian majority. They promptly restored the House of Lords and accepted Charles' conciliatory Declaration of Breda. On May 29 Charles II triumphantly rode into London.

Nedham had been ousted from his editorship a year before this climactic event. Ten months before it he published <u>Interest will not Lie. Or, a View of England's True Interest: In reference to the Papist. Royalist. Presbyterian. Baptised. Neuter. Army. Parliament. City of London.</u> Both its format and its organization intentionally recalled his tentatively Royalist <u>Case of the Kingdom</u> of 1647. But in this fifty-page signed anti-Royalist tract Nedham was not tentative, though now he was even more obviously whistling in the dark.

He begins with the Catholics: only they will benefit from a restoration of the monarchy, for Charles I "first laid the foundations of our Civil Wars" in their behalf. In the remaining sections Nedham, after briefly answering John Fell's monarchist <u>The Interest of England Stated</u>, adjusts his argument to the self-interest of each of his target groups. Cleverly he tries to divide the Royalists into two factions: those who support the monarchy for reasons of "necessity," and those who support it for reasons of "humour." The second group is much larger, and it is they who will gain economically, politically, and religiously by maintaining stability and rejecting Charles II. It is "but folly to embroil their Country, and engage all that is dear to them, for the old form, which is in itself a mere shadow, and like a shadow goes away."

As for the Presbyterians: a restored monarchy will enable "the Episcopacie" again to oppress them, and Charles's son will be especially vindictive. Moreover, their oath to the crown (the Solemn League and Covenant) has been superseded by their Engagement to support the Commonwealth. Could your earlier oath, Nedham asks, "die or take a nap...and [then] revive?" Similarly, it is to the self-interest of the Baptists not to allow a persecuting king to be enthroned--and again Nedham skillfully plays the like-father-like-son refrain.

"The Neuter, a great part of the Nation," should be aware of the power of the army, fearful about imminent tumults and worried about higher taxes. "The Yong Man [Charles II] hath innumerable vast debts contracted by him beyond Sea; these must be paid too, and which way (I pray you) but out of the General Purse."

Nedham then flatters the army, reiterates that Charles II is not to be trusted, and implores the soldiers, for their own preservation, to stick with Parliament. Only that way will they ever receive the pay due them.

The longest section of <u>Interest will not Lie</u> is reserved for wooing Parliament. The reduced Rump, Nedham claims, is free and representative. In a distorted survey of Interregnum history he almost makes a convincing case that those MPs who had been excluded should have been, that the Rump has behaved like--and been accepted as--a proper legislative assembly, and that it is now the real de facto power in England. Almost, but not quite. In his involved argument Nedham repeatedly attacks Prynne, buffeting him with historical and scriptural examples, passages from Hugo Grotius, and the anti-Royalist statements of a prominent Presbyterian divine, Richard Baxter. But it is tough sledding, and one paragraph can indicate the lengths to which Nedham was prepared to go in his legalistic and sophistic rhetoric:

> As to the grand Argument which both our Author [John Fell], Mr. Pryn, and others doe

use, that according to Law the Parliament was dissolved by the Kings death: Tis true, that it was so provided by Law, that the death of a King dissolved a Parliament; but you are to observe that this was a Law relating to the Constitution of Parliament in the ordinary Course of its regulation, and respecting only the formality of the Writ summoning the Parliament to advise with the particular person of the King in whose name the writ was issued forth; and truly when the old Constitution remained without disturbance, it was reason it should be retained in its ordinary course; but in an extraordinary case, as that of this Parliament hath been in all the great revolutions from first to last, when the very Constitution, Parliamentary itself as to the nature of the Powers and Rights of the several parties, King and people therein concerned, fell under Question, and when the sword was drawn betwixt the parties to decide it, and the King persisted to claim the whole Right of Soveraignty contrary to that antient Constitution, and referred his Claim to the determination of the sword, and thereby according to the equity of our fundamental Laws, forfeited his Kingship, and became a private person, dissolved the Constitution of the Kingdom, introduced another Law, viz, the Law of Arms, to try his Cause by, and pleaded with sword in hand to the very last, is it reason in such an extraordinary Case as this, that the surviving party of that King should ground an Argument upon the formalities and ordinary usages of a Constitution, whenas that Constitution it self hath by the King himself been dissolved long agoe?

Nedham, when he had no other recourse, could be as dull and pedantic as William Prynne.[114]

      <u>Interest will not Lie</u> concludes with an appeal to the City of London. Again Nedham opens with flattery, then goes on to describe the revenge Charles II will exact, including the spectre

of repression by the Catholics in his entourage, and ends with the pocketbook argument that a Restoration will cripple London's domestic and foreign trade. "It is easie to guess what will become of that, when it shall be counted Reason of State to keep you poor and low."

As *The Case of the Kingdom* failed to halt Charles's journey to the scaffold, so *Interest will not Lie* failed to halt his son's journey to the throne. But Nedham did not give up. When he was fired as editor of *Politicus* and the *Intelligencer* he tried to compete with his successor by means of an eight-page weekly, *The Moderate Informer*. Bland and cautious, it closed--or was closed--after two numbers. But *Interest will not Lie* boosted his stock with the republicans and the militant army leaders. Shortly after its publication they reinstated Nedham as editor of the two official weeklies. Canne, during these intervening three months, had made few changes, and Nedham took over approximately where he had left off. But the political winds were shifting and Nedham began to trim his journalistic sails, though he could not lower them. He had been so long and so closely identified with Cromwell that he could neither embrace nor be embraced by the Royalists. As their cause gained strength, however, he became more palatable to the radicals. So Nedham continued to battle against the Restoration and for the Good Old Cause. The evidence of this battle is clear if infrequent in his two weeklies. In November 1659, for instance, his obituary on Bradshaw included high praise for this "Noblest Friend" who had wisely presided over the trial of Charles I.[115] Milton, too, was still manning the anti-Royalist barricades, and it is pleasant to note that Bradshaw, in a 1655 codicil to his will, bequeathed ₤10 each to Nedham and Milton.[116]

Several times at the end of the year Nedham criticized Monk as a covert Royalist, and he opposed the readmission to Parliament of those who had been excluded in 1648.[117] In December in the *Intelligencer* he printed a short attack on the monarchy, then in *Politicus* defended his right to take such a stand, though his defense was subdued.[118] Gradually thereafter he further reefed his sails. Accounts of Charles II now appeared more frequently, and Nedham increasingly portrayed him as a potential king, decreasingly as a wandering minstrel. During the early months of 1660 story after story acknowledged the growth of sentiment for the Restoration. Monk began to dominate the news, and Nedham now depicted him as an intelligent if close-mouthed patriot. Yet until the very end Nedham dropped veiled hints that his heart was still with the Good Old Cause.

During the final month of Nedham's tenure as editor his two weeklies became almost totally safe and inoffensive. Their foreign news remained relatively reliable and extensive, and they treated domestic events with brevity and circumspection. Even so, his sun was setting. His ₤100 subsidy from the government came to an end in 1659. The circulation of both papers shrank, mainly because of competition from a variety of revived semi-official and Royalist journals, partly because of their loss of vigor and of inside information.[119] The number of advertisements diminished proportionately. The last few numbers of *Mercurius Politicus* and *The Publick Intelligencer* were full of items about prominent Londoners who were eagerly repudiating their actions against the monarchy. On April 9, 1660 the Council of State "discharged Nedham from writing the weekly Intelligence, and order'd Dury and Muddiman to do it."[120] (In November, the wheel having come full circle, Berkenhead, now Sir John, was appointed their official licenser.)[121] The final issue of *Politicus* edited by Nedham came out on April 9, of the *Intelligencer* three days later.[122] Charles II had issued his Declaration from Breda on April 4.

Perhaps because his restricted editorial job had become boring, perhaps because he wanted to go out with more of a bang than a whimper, perhaps because of conviction, Nedham on March 10 published a short pamphlet, Newes From Brussels. In a Letter From A Neer Attendant On His Majesties Person. According to Wood, it was "conveyed to the printer or bookseller by that notorious schismatic and grand zealot for the good old cause called Praise-God Barebone."[123] The Council of State immediately offered a reward of ₤20 for the apprehension of the allegedly anonymous author.[124] The diarist John Evelyn recorded his anger at "a wicked forg'd paper, pretended to be sent from Bruxells to defame his Majesties person and vertues, and render him odious, now when every body was in hope and expectation of the General [Monk] and Parliament recalling him, and establishing the Government on its antient and right basis." In fact, Evelyn was angry enough to recover quickly from an illness and quickly to write his own confused rebuttal, The Late News... from Bruxels Unmasked.[125]

Nedham's Epitaph on the Duke of Hamilton is on a par with Dryden's satiric poetry; his Newes From Brussels is almost on a par with Swift's satiric prose. Adopting the persona of a Cavalier, the author excoriates the Presbyterians and recommends to the King that you should "Hug them that you cannot hang, at least until you can." Meanwhile, this laughing Cavalier reports, the King has ordered us to be "plaguy-godly" to the Presbyterians, though he has trouble hiding his own laughter when they preach to and at him. Nedham then ridicules the reliability of royal promises, especially promises of mercy: "Tush! remember that blessed line of Machiavel; he's an oafe that thinks an oath, or any other tender, can tame a prince beyond his pleasure." The blood of Charles I cries out for revenge, and all those directly or indirectly responsible for his beheading must be exterminated. Indeed, all of England will have to "submit tamely to the halter."

Nedham does more than to express what were the true sentiments of many Royalists; he also captures the trivial and conspiratorial tone of those who had spent ten years in exile--and he obviously took delight in his parody:

> O Jesu, Jack! I want an iron hook to keep my sides form splitting, to see my Prince bite his lips for halfe an hour long, while that Dulmano begs a blessing (as he calls it) as our Mock-beggers do their Bacon at the Farmers door. G. got behinde him yesterday and made mouths, which the Puppy by an unhappy turn of his head perceived; but his Majestie seeing all, prudently accepted his complaint, and with a Royal Gravity, not onely rebuked G. but immediately dismist him his service.
> We all made application to the Parson to mediate to our Master for G. his restoration...M.H. and J. were in the presence at night, but I thought we should have all split our spleenes a laughing....H. bid me hand his service to thee, he swears he hath horn'd 15 Cuckolds within these 14 dayes....Bid Phil and's brother be close....

Nedham's concluding sentence in this Letter, "which casually became thus publique," is at once sarcastic and sinister: "Get Arms, but buy them not in such suspicious numbers: that if all fails, we may repair to them, and cut our passage to the Throne through Traitors blood. Farewel."

Nedham's own farewell was orchestrated by a chorus of Royalist catcalls. But in the spring of 1659, almost a year before he fled England, he had been attacked from the left. <u>A True Catalogue, Or, An Account of the Several Places and most Eminent Persons...where and by whom Richard Cromwell was Proclaimed Lord Protector</u> can serve as an appropriately ambiguous epitaph to Nedham's service as Cromwell's press agent. It itemizes "the most material passages in the several blasphemous, lying, flattering addresses" to Oliver's son. Relying on <u>Mercurius Politicus</u>, the republican author lists ninety-four of these addresses but admits that there were more. He then claims that this outpouring of expressions of loyalty was arranged by John Thurloe and by that "old malignant pamphleteer, that lying railing Rabshekah, and defamer," Marchamont Nedham. As his evidence he cites the similarities in language and substance of the addresses to Richard Cromwell from a wide variety of groups and places.[126]

This accusation could be true. Thurloe and Nedham had long worked together, and both were capable of concocting and implementing a scheme like this. On the other hand, such expressions of loyalty tended to be formalized and homogenized. Also, since at the start Richard Cromwell's succession was peaceful and popular, no outside push was needed to generate these addresses. But the verdict is ambiguous. Not ambiguous is the conclusion of <u>A True Catalog</u>, in which Nedham is characterized as a time-server, "odius to almost everybody...[who] prostrates...[his] Learning, Conscience, Credit, and Pen, to serve the interests and lusts of a few corrupt men."

This was the only attack on Nedham at the end of his journalistic career by a supporter of the Good Old Cause. During his final months as editor the recently revived Royalist weeklies delighted in calling him a liar and a traitor and gloating over his misfortunes.[127] Several pamphlets echoed them. On the first day of 1660 the London public was greeted with a broadside by W. Kilbourne: <u>A New Years-Gift For Mercurius Politicus</u>. In mediocre verse it attacks Nedham both as a journalist and as the author of <u>Interest will not Lie</u>: "He writes against the Cavaliers,/ He pulls the Presbyterians ears." In May <u>A Rope for Pol. Or, A Hue and Cry after Marchamont Nedham</u> had on its title-page the biblical passage, "Shall not Shimei be put to death?"; and 'To the Reader' advocates that he "who hath with so much malice calumniated his Sovereign, so scurrilously abused the Nobility, so impudently blasphemed the Church, and so industriously poysoned the people with dangerous principles, should (at least) carry some sort of mark about him." Then follow forty pages of short anti-Royalist quotations from <u>Mercurius</u>

Politicus. But the anonymous author badly miscalculated: his Rope for Pol turns out to be a necklace, a string of passages which display Nedham at his wittiest and most incisive.

A verse broadside of that spring did not miscalculate. It is as blunt and direct as its title:

<u>The Downfall of Mercurius</u> (<u>Britanicus</u>
(<u>Pragmaticus</u>
(<u>Politicus</u>

Despite the earlier successes of this "Three-Head Cerberus,"

> ...now the time is coming which no doubt
> Will do him justice, vengeance will find him out.

And the author concludes:

> Thus with the times he turned. Next time I hope
> Will up the ladder be and down the rope.

Even more heavy-handed and vindictive was a short tract in prose: <u>A Dialogue between Thomas Scot and Marchamont Nedham</u>. Scot was executed as a regicide in the autumn of 1660, and the author of <u>A Dialogue</u> must have relished the spectacle-- except that Nedham was not accompanying Scot. At about the same time, <u>The Character of the Rump</u> lists Nedham, "The Commonwealth didapper," as being on the same roster with Milton of those who are "to travel to Tyburn" and the scaffold.[128] As a final fitting touch, for two weeks late in the spring a newspaper named <u>Mercurius Aulicus</u> gloated over Nedham's plight.[129]

Nedham was by now fully aware that a rope or an ax was waiting for him. At the very end of April 1660 he fled to Holland.[130]

Footnotes   Chapter IV

1. It is dated Aug. 1, 1649, but it is one of the very few works published in England between 1640 and 1661 which is not in the Thomason Collection. Hence the date on which it actually came out cannot be verified, though early August seems correct. I am assuming that Nedham was not the "M.N." who contributed an elegy on Henry, Lord Hastings to Lachrymae Musarum. Hastings died on June 24, 1649, and this commemorative volume, containing Dryden's first published poem, came out a few months later. It seems to me unlikely that Nedham, now in jail, would have written anything so intricate and hyperbolic, not to mention so politically unremunerative. For futher details see The Works of John Dryden, ed. Edward Niles Hooker and H.T. Swedenberg, Jr., Berkeley: University of California Press, 1956, I, 172f.; and Frank, Hobbled Pegasus, pp. 248f.

2. Wood, p. 1181.

3. Calendar of State Papers, Domestic, 1649-50, p. 554; Firth, DNB.

4. James Heath, A Brief Chronicle of the Late Intestine War, "The Second Impression greatly enlarged," London, 1663, p. 492, says that Bradshaw "hired" Nedham, "a jack of all sides transcendently gifted in opprobrious and treasonable Droll...to act the second part to his starcht and more solemn Treason."

5. Calendar of State Papers, Domestic, 1650, p. 174.

6. For a functional and incisive discussion of the Engagement Controversy see John M. Wallace, Destiny His Choice: The Loyalism

128

of Andrew Marvell, Cambridge: at the University Press, 1968, pp. 43-68. See also Knachel, Case, xii-xiv.

7. Gardiner, Commonwealth and Protectorate, I, 193. For a summary of some of these serious polemics see Wallace Destiny, pp. 44-66; and Knachel, Case, pp. xxvii-xxxii.

8. Knachel, Case, p. 3. The page references to The Case which follow are to Knachel's edition.

9. Knachel, Case, p. 4.

10. Knachel, Case, pp. 13f.

11. Knachel, Case, p. 28.

12. Knachel, Case, pp. 28f. For a discussion of the background to this power-of-the-sword argument, see Knachel, Case, pp. xxvi-xxxi. The Case's marginal citations show that Nedham had done his homework thoroughly in regard to the Engagement Controversy.

13. Knachel, Case, p. 31.

14. Knachel, Case, p. 40.

15. Knachel, Case, pp. 41f.

16. Knachel, Case, p. 70.

17. Knachel, Case, p. 71.

18. Knachel, Case, p.77.

19. Knachel, Case, p. 83.

20. Knachel, Case, p. 88.

21. Knachel, Case, p. 91.

22. Knachel, Case, p. 94.

23. Knachel, <u>Case</u>, p. 102.

24. Knachel, <u>Case</u>, p. 110.

25. Knachel, <u>Case</u>, p. 120.

26. Knachel, <u>Case</u>, p. 123.

27. Knachel, <u>Case</u>, pp. 127f.

28. Knachel, <u>Case</u>, p. 126. Early in 1651 R.F. (R. Fletcher?) published three separate poems which parallel Nedham's might-makes-right support of the Commonwealth: <u>Mercurius Heliconicus</u>, <u>Mercurius Heliconicus, Numb. 2</u>, and <u>Radius Heliconicus</u>. They are worthy of note here because R.F. seems very like Nedham in his cynicism, pragmatism, flexibility, wit, and skill. (For further details see Frank, <u>Hobbled Pegasus</u>, pp. 273-277.)

29. An anonymous pamphlet of late Oct. 1650 satirizes Nedham, and indirectly mentions this appendix: <u>The Second Character of Mercurius Politicus</u>. (See French, "Milton, Needham, and 'Politicus'," pp. 204f.)

30. Davis Masson, <u>The Life of John Milton</u>, reprinted New York: Peter Smith, 1946, IV, 89.

31. J. Milton French, <u>The Life Records of John Milton</u>, New Brunswick: Rutgers University Press, 1949-1958, III, 9; Knachel, <u>Case</u>, p. xxviii. Milton may have performed this nominal task for a longer period. Earlier, the weekly had been registered "by permission of authority," and the authority could have been Milton. After Jan. 22, 1652, <u>Politicus</u> was for almost a year entered in the Stationers' Register without the name of any licenser. For the detailed story of the registration of <u>Politicus</u> to mid-1654, see William Riley Parker, <u>Milton-A Biography</u>,

31. (cont.) Oxford: At the Clarendon Press, 1968, pp. 993f.

32. French, Life Records, II, 278.

33. E.g., Masson, Milton, IV, 326f. H. Sylvia Anthony, "Mercurius Politicus Under Milton," Journal of the History of Ideas, XXVII (1966), 593-609, makes a case for Milton's direct if limited influence on many of the editorials in Mercurius Politicus. I agree with her conclusions concerning when and how Nedham's The Excellencie Of A Free State was written, and her article has several usable facts and insights. But in regard to Milton's influence, I find her unconvincing.

34. Frank, BN, p. 200.

35. Frank, BN, pp. 200-203.

36. Frank, BN, p. 205.

37. Frank, BN, p. 207. French, Life Records, III, 310ff. The prospectus also said cryptically that the editor would "sayle in a middle way, between the Scylla and Charybdis of Scurrility and prophanes." Occasionally in the early 1900's the editorship of Mercurius Politicus was attributed to John Hall. Nedham's editorship is, however, irrefutable.

38. Newcomb remained the printer until the demise of Politicus in 1660. He also printed its companion, The Publick Intelligencer, The Case of the Commonwealth, and Interest will not Lie--and for this he was jeered at, in September 1660, in The London Printer His Lamentation. (See French, Life Records, IV, 336.) Newcomb also was the printer of Nedham's The Great Accuser Cast Down.

39. Frank, BN, p. 207.

40. Heath, Brief Chronicle, p. 492.

41. A Rope for Pol, London, 1660. Wood was so impressed with this comment that he incorporated it verbatim in his biography of Nedham.

42. Knachel, Case, p. xxxvi.

43. Anthony, "Mercurius Politicus Under Milton," pp. 602f.

44. French, "Milton, Needham, and 'Politicus'," p. 242.

45. See note 33, above.

46. J.G.A. Pocock, The Machiavellian Moment, Princeton: Princeton University Press, 1975, p. 382.

47. Excellencie, p. 13.

48. Excellencie, p. 19.

49. Excellencie, p. 35.

50. Excellencie, pp. 45f.

51. Excellencie, p. 54.

52. Excellencie, p. 64.

53. Excellencie, p. 76.

54. Excellencie, p. 94.

55. Excellencie, pp. 99f.

56. Excellencie, pp. 145f.

57. Excellencie, p. 161.

58. Excellencie, p. 244.

59. It is worth noting, however, that in May 1652 Lilburne, then in exile in Amsterdam, in a self-vindication entitled As You Were, praises Milton's 'First Defense' and Mercurius Politicus. (See Frank, Levellers, p. 230; Parker, Milton, p. 1016.)

60. Quoted in Anthony, "Mercurius Politicus Under Milton," p. 602.

61. Knachel, Case, p. xi.

62. Peter Shaw, The Character of John Adams, New York: W.W. Norton & Company, Inc., 1977, pp. 219f.; Anthony, "Mercurius Politicus Under Milton," p. 604. The copy read by Adams was entitled The Right Constitution of a Commonwealth, and Nedham's name appears on the title-page. My thanks to my colleague, Everett Emerson, for telling me about John Adams' knowledge of Nedham.

63. Mercurius Politicus, nos. 352-355, March 5-Apr. 2, 1652. See Also Firth, Last Years, pp. 155-161; and Wilbur C. Abbot, The Writings and Speeches of Oliver Cromwell, Cambridge: Harvard University Press, 1937-1947, IV, 431.

64. Quoted in Masson, Milton, V, 659.

65. Most of this material concerning Milton and Mercurius Politicus comes from French, "Milton, Needham, and 'Mercurius Politicus'," pp. 242-252.

66. According to Wood, p. 1188, these "additional Evidences" were procured from John Bradshaw.

67. Bound with both copies of this book that I have seen is a 37-page supplement, translated from the Italian, entitled 'Dominium Maris: Or, The Dominion of the Sea.' It concerns the right of Venice to control the

67. (cont.) Adriatic, and the preliminary 'To the Reader' draws a parallel between English and Venetian maritime rights. Thomason picked it up as a separate tract on May 25, 1652, and I see no reason to attribute it to Nedham, who as far as I know did not speak Italian. The brief 'To the Reader' could be his.

68. Calendar of State Papers, Domestic, 1652-53, p. 486. Assuming my transcription thereof is correct, Firth's figure of ₤200 in DNB is wrong. The book's translation was re-edited and the original dedication restored by James Howell in 1662. Earlier, on Oct. 14, 1650, the Council of State had "instructed" Nedham "to put into Latin the treatise he wrote in answer to a Spanish piece in defense of the murderers of Mr. Ascham." (Calendar of State Papers, Domestic 1650, p. 387. Firth DNB; Masson, Milton, IV, 229.) I have been unable to locate a copy, or even any record, of this purported treatise or its Latin translation. Prof. John M. Perlette of the University of Florida, who is working on a biography of Ascham, informs me that he can find "no record of or reference to the Nedham treatise."

69. Calendar of State Papers, Domestic, 1654, pp. 447, 449, 455, 458; 1655, pp. 127, 604; 1655-56, pp. 585, 586; 1656-57, pp. 591f.; 1657-58, pp. 556f.; 1658-59, p. 584.

70. Frank, BN, p. 223.

71. Parker, Milton, p. 994.

72. Among the more obvious trial balloons were reports in Mercurius Politicus of peace feelers from Holland so that the Council of State could test the London reaction (no. 107, June 17-24, 1652; no. 147, March 31-Apr. 7, 1653).

73. This paragraph is based on data scattered throughout Frank, BN.

74. Politicus, no. 97, Apr. 8-15, 1652.

75. Clyde, Freedom of the Press, p. 246; Politicus, no. 224, Sept. 21-28, 1654.

76. E.g., Politicus, no. 222, Sept. 7-14, 1654; no. 246, Feb. 22-March 1, 1655; no. 219, Aug. 17-24, 1654.

77. Politicus, no. 208, June 1-8, 1654.

78. Politicus, no. 221, Aug. 24-31, 1654.

79. Politicus, no. 257, May 10-17, 1655; no. 180, Nov. 17-24, 1653; no. 215, July 20-27, 1654; no. 236, Dec. 14-21, 1654; no. 247, March 1-8, 1655.

80. Frank, BN, p. 246.

81. Cited in J.G. Muddiman, The King's Journalist 1659-1689, London: The Bodley Head, 1923, p. 125.

82. Masson, Milton, V, 180.

83. On Feb. 8, 1654, a 52-page tract entitled A True State of the Case of the Commonwealth, in reference to the late Established Government by a Lord Protector and a Parliament appeared. Firth (Last Years, p. 156), Abbot (Cromwell, III, 193), and Ivan Roots (Commonwealth and Protectorate, New York: Schocken Books, 1966, pp. 170f.) attribute it to Nedham. Wallace (Destiny His Choice, p. 113) is neutral. Knachel does not mention this tract and Wing does not list it under Nedham. The title and the timing suggest Nedham's authorship, as does the likelihood that A True State was commissioned by Thurloe. The author condemns the Nominated Parliament, which Cromwell

83. (cont.) dismissed in December 1653, and supports the Instrument of Government, which established the Protectorate. He exaggerates the republican potential of that Instrument, as well as its "unitive virtue," he appeals to English traditionalism and patriotism, and at one point he equates Cromwell's role with God's: "It was high time some power should pass upon the wavering humours of the people, and say to the Nation as the Almnighty said once to the unruly sea, Here shall be thy bounds, hitherto shalt thou come, and no further." A True State thus defends a return to monarchy--with Cromwell as king. I am, however, as certain as I can be that Nedham did not write it. I do not base this on the content, for every conservative sentiment in A True Case Nedham was then capable of uttering. I base it on the pamphlet's style--and I forced myself to read it twice. That style is too dull, bland, homogenized, and long-winded to be his: possibly in a short tract, but not for fifty-two pages. Also, there are lengthy pious stretches which are not in his vein, nor is the author's use of the impersonal and grandiose "we." It thus strikes me as most unlikely that the long, loose, and often rambling sentences which make up most of A True Case would have dripped from Nedham's pen. As a postscript to support my negative case: there is no record of Nedham's receiving an extra stipend for performing this chore.

84. Calendar of State Papers, Domestic, 1653-54, pp. 304-308.

85. Calendar of State Papers, Domestic, 1653-54, p. 306; Abbot, Cromwell, III, 147.

86. Known as the "tub-preacher," Hannah Trapnel had been impressing large crowds with her trances and revelations; and she made much of recent marvels, omens, and prodigies

86. (cont.) which demonstrated God's dislike of the Protectorate.

87. Calendar of State Papers, Domestic, 1653-54, p. 393. See also Abbot, Cromwell, III, 193, and Muddiman, King's Journalist, p. 34.

88. Calendar of State Papers, Domestic, 1655, p. 139; A Collection of the State Papers of John Thurloe, ed. Thomas Birch, London, 1742, pp. 483-85.

89. Calendar of State Papers, Domestic, 1656-57, p. 318; Abbot, Cromwell, IV, 432.

90. G.E. Aylmer, Ed., The Interregnum: The Quest for Settlement 1640-1660, London: Macmillan, 1972, p. 178 (from David Underdown, "Settlement in the Counties 1653-1658").

91. There is a functional biography of Goodwin in DNB by Alexander Gordon.

92. Thomas Jackson, The Life of John Goodwin, London: Longmans, Green, Reader, and Dyer, 1872, p. 375. See also Benjamin Hanbury, Historical Memorials Relating to the Independents, London, 1844, III, 432ff.

93. Jackson, Goodwin, p. 375; Wood, p. 1186.

94. Nedham, Great Accuser, p. 99.

95. Nedham, Great Accuser, pp. 64-66.

96. Jackson, Goodwin, pp. 375ff.; Clyde, Freedom of the Press, p. 290; Wood, p. 1186. The title of Goodwin's book which includes the reply to Nedham is Triumviri. In the Preface Goodwin accuses Nedham of having "a foul mouth, which Satan hath opened against the truth and mind of God," and as being "a person of an infamous and unclean character." (Quoted in Firth, DNB.)

97. Donald Wing, *A Gallery of Ghosts*, New York: Modern Language Association, 1967: *The Trial* is listed under Nedham, and Wood attributes it to him.

98. Abbot, *Cromwell*, III, 837; Christopher Hill, *God's Englishman: Oliver Cromwell and the English Revolution*, New York: The Dial Press, 1970, p. 150. Clyde, *Freedom of the Press*, p. 247 reports that at least one English ambassador complained to Thurloe about the inaccuracy of some of the foreign news in *Mercurius Politicus*.

99. Masson, *Milton*, V, 352.

100. Frank, *BN*, p. 359.

101. *Politicus*, no. 399, Jan. 14-21, 1658. This and other items, including advertisements, can usually be found, in identical form, in the appropriate number of *The Publick Intelligencer*.

102. *Politicus*, no. 326, Sept. 4-11, 1656; no. 402, Feb. 4-11, 1658; no. 566 (the paper had recently and unaccountably jumped from #455 to #545 in its numbering), May 5-12, 1659.

103. E.G., *Politicus*, no. 407, March 11-18, 1658.

104. E.G., *Politicus*, nos. 286-289, Nov. 29-Dec. 27, 1655; no. 293, Jan. 17-24, 1656; no. 340, Dec. 11-18, 1656; no. 408, March 18-25, 1658; no. 547, Dec. 23-30, 1658.

105. *Politicus*, no. 300, March 6-13, 1656; no. 424, June 24-July 1, 1658.

106. *Politicus*, no. 379, Aug. 27-Sept. 3, 1657; no. 443, Nov. 18-25, 1658.

107. *Politicus*, no. 432, Sept. 2-9, 1658.

108. E.G., *Politicus*, no. 291, Jan. 3-10, 1656; no. 305, Apr. 10-17, 1656; no. 355, March 26-Apr. 2, 1657; no. 358, Apr. 16-23, 1657.

109. *Politicus*, no. 381, Sept. 10-17, 1657; no. 335, Nov. 6-13, 1656.

110. *Politicus*, no. 329, Sept. 25-Oct. 2, 1656.

111. *Politicus*, no. 346, Jan. 22-29, 1657; no. 435, Sept. 23-30, 1658; no. 547, Dec. 23-30, 1658; no. 439, Oct. 21-28, 1658; no. 550, Jan. 13-20, 1659; no. 442, Nov. 11-18, 1658.

112. *Politicus*, no. 382, Sept. 17-24, 1658; no. 387, Oct. 22-29, 1658.

113. *Politicus*, no. 555, Feb. 17-24, 1659.

114. Pyrnne's predictable answer appeared in November: *A Brief, Necessary Vindication of the Old and New Secluded Members*. Earlier, in May 1659, he had attacked Milton and Nedham as subversives, in *A True and Perfect Narrative*. (See French, *Life Records*, IV, 266.)

115. *Politicus*, no. 592 (the second issue so numbered), Oct. 27-Nov. 3, 1659.

116. Masson, *Milton*, V, 630. According to both *DNB* and *Politicus* Bradshaw died on Oct. 31, not, as Masson says, on Nov. 22.

117. E.g., *Politicus*, no. 595, Nov. 17-24, 1659; no. 598, Dec. 8-15, 1659.

118. *Publick Intelligencer*, no. 207, Dec. 12-19, 1659; *Politicus*, no. 599, Dec. 15-22, 1659.

119. Frank, *BN*, pp. 259-266; Davies, *Restoration of Charles II*, pp. 118f.

120. Bulstrode Whitelock, *Memorials of English Affairs*, Oxford: at the University Press,

120. (cont.) 1853, IV, 406. Henry Muddiman, the most important journalist of the early 1660's, had become intimate with Monk, and later he and Pepys became friends. Like Nedham, Muddiman was skilled, energetic, flexible; and he was the first allegedly neutral journalist openly to jump on the Restoration bandwagon. Pepys characterized him as "a good scholar and an arch rogue." Giles Dury, probably a Scot, quickly withdrew from the newspaper scene.

121. Masson, *Milton*, VI, 202.

122. It is very possible that *Politicus* and *The Publick Intelligencer* were not edited by Nedham that final week. A letter dated Apr. 5, 1660 reports that he had run away. (Francis Newport to Sir Richard Leveson: in *Historical Manuscripts Commission*, Fifth *Report*, p. 149.)

123. Wood, p. 1187; Masson, *Milton*, V, 671f. Masson adds that the pamphlet "was attributed at once to Nedham."

124. Davies, *Restoration of Charles II*, p. 314.

125. Geoffrey, Keynes, *John Evelyn*, New York: The Grolier Club, 1937, p. 78. Evelyn's reply to Nedham is often sloppily sentimental, and his eulogy of Charles II borders on parody: "His person so lovely, amiable, and gratefull...so meek, gentle, and sweet of Behaviour; so firm, constant, and obliging in his Friendships...but above all, so firmly and irremovably fixed to the profession of the true Protestant Religion." (Quoted in Davies, *Restoration of Charles II*, p. 316.) Evelyn was more irritated by Nedham's "Drollery" than by his allegations that the Royalists are vengeful, greedy, etc. That Nedham wrote the unsigned *Newes from Brussels* was acknowledged by several of his contemporaries. See also Davies, *Restoration of Charles II*, pp. 315f.

126. Davies, <u>Restoration of Charles II</u>, p. 11, and David Underdown, <u>Pride's Purge: Politics in the Puritan Revolution</u>, Oxford: at the Clarendon Press, 1971, p. 344, repeat this allegation.

127. Frank, <u>BN</u>, p. 266; Davies, <u>Restoration of Charles II</u>, pp. 118f, 170f.

128. Early in April <u>Treason Arraigned</u> also linked Milton and Nedham, "his brother Rabshakeh," and suggested that each "come hang yourself." (See Masson, <u>Milton</u>, V, 665f.)

129. Even the Royalist astrologer George Wharton got into the act: his <u>A Second Narrative of the Late Parliament (so called)</u> refers to Nedham as, among other things, "that foul-mouth'd Malignant."

130. Masson, <u>Milton</u>, V, 702.

CHAPTER V

FOURTH MOVEMENT -- 1660-1678

On May 10, 1660 a verse broadside appeared in London: <u>O. Cromwells Thankes to the Lord Generall [Monk] ....Together with an Hue and Cry after Mercurius Politicus.</u> Three stanzas are relevant to Nedham:

> But if at Amsterdam you meet
> With one that's purblind in the street,
> Hawk-nos'd--turn up his hair,
> And in his eares two holes you'll finde,
> And (if they are not pawned) behinde
> Two rings are hanging there.
>
> His visage meagre is and long--
> His body slender, but his tongue
> If once you chance to hear,
> Observe it well, it has a grace
> Becoming no such traitor's face
> Of English, that are there.
>
> Some forty years he is of age,
> In's prime to act on any stage
> And fit for any plot.
> Had he not been of Oxfordshire,
> Because he writes so much for hire,
> I'd swear he was a Scot.[1]

One can be skeptical about the pawnable earrings, but the verse shows that Nedham was in Amsterdam, and it implies that he was not suffering from either depression or poverty. Wood confirms that money was not a problem: In September, Nedham, "for money given to an hungry courtier, obtained his pardon under the great seal," and returned to London.[2] Wood is a little vague on dates, but on August 29 Charles signed the Bill of Indemnity, from which Nedham, surprisingly, was not excluded; and in October a fly-by-night London weekly reported that "There is lately come to town that subtile sophister, Mar--- Ned---, Oliver's vindicator, the metropolitan pamphleteer."[3]

Wood goes on to show that Nedham's pardon was worth whatever he paid for it. At Oxford, in 1661, "several set upon him in St. Mary's church to hale him before a justice, and so to prison for treason: so that...being free, and at liberty by virtue of that seal, which he several times produced," he got away; and thereafter apparently he was not molested. (Nedham's former boss, John Thurloe, incidentally, had no such troubles. Because the Restoration government needed his knowledge of and memoranda about foreign affairs, his life was spared and he was promptly put to work.)[4] Wood then concludes his narrative of the events in Nedham's life: "He exercised the faculty of physic to his dying day among the brethren, which was a considerable benefit to him."[5] Nedham undoubtedly prospered, and probably his clientele soon included Royalists along with the ailing brethren of the moribund Good Old Cause.

Nedham was not the type who relished political exile and he quickly tried to work his way back toward the centers of power. In April 1661 he published a signed broadside: The Cities Feast To The Lord Protector. Its thirteen stanzas, to be sung to the tune of 'Cooke Lorrell,' are conventionally anti-Cromwell:

> Then His Highness commanded the Mayor to kneel,
> The Beast of the City was soon on his knees,
> He made him a Knight with Iron and Steel,
> And Bid him rise up, and pay him his fees.
> With a ran tan the Devil is dead.

A short time later Nedham tried again, this time much more elaborately repudiating his political career during the 1650's and recalling his role as a Royalist during the late 1640's. The title of this effort is self-explanatory: A Short History of the English rebellion. Compiled in Verse, by Marchamont Nedham; And formerly extant, in his Weekly Mercurius Pragmaticus.[6] It is an impressive tour de force in its attempt to recapture the mood of what then must have seemed at once a very remote and a very recent past. The 'History' consists of 256 four-line stanzas: the sixty-four title-page poems from Mercurius Pragmaticus between Sept. 14, 1647 and Dec. 26, 1648.[7] A Short History therefore belongs mainly to an earlier period of Nedham's life, and these weekly poems, especially when they are heaped together, reveal Nedham's facility in doggerel and invective, his enjoyment of political infighting, and his flexibility. They also reveal his loyalty to Charles I during the sixteen months preceding his trial and execution. But Charles II was not impressed. Nedham continued, full time, his practice of medicine. Yet, according to Wood, A Short History was reprinted in 1680, "when the presbyterians were busy to carry on their designs under the pretence of the Popish Plot."[8]

In April 1663 Nedham remarried. His second wife was a widow, Elizabeth Thompson, ten years younger than he.[9] He also retained some contact with Milton, though after the Restoration his visits to the blind poet were probably infrequent.[10] A month after his second marriage he published a thoroughly safe and domesticated tract: A Discourse Concerning Schools and School-Masters. Nedham begins it by praising "our late blessed and wonderful Restauration" and castigating the "late villainous changes" of the Interregnum. He devotes two of his sixteen pages to criticizing non-conformist schools, and in the interests of orthodoxy he proposes the exclusion from teaching of "schismatics." Is it consistent, he asks, "to banish schism out of the church and to countenance it in the schools?" And his concluding sentence urges the established church "to recover those persons [school teachers] to a sound Orthodox Sense, whose Childhood hath been poysoned and prepossessed with Schism."

Despite these reactionary sentiments, his language is generally mild and his main pitch is for higher salaries for teachers. Many academics would agree with his contention that "'Tis the salary which makes Schools and Learning flourish." Other points in A Discourse are equally noncontroversial. Nedham advocates starting education at an early age, encouraging uniformity in methods of teaching as productive of better pedagogy and less schism, and training more, as well as more highly specialized, teachers to staff the growing number of schools the country needs. In passing, he recommends that whippping should be used very sparingly if at all. Though his tract urges that it is the Anglican Bishops who are to supervise the raising of standards and the maintenance of uniformity, the major thrust of A Discourse is that teachers are overworked and underpaid.[11]

One ironic sentence from it may have been written with the author's tongue very deep in his cheeck: "If these schismatic schoolmasters were given by the vicar-general licence to practice physic instead of teach schools," England would be better off. Since the Restoration Nedham had been excluded from playing a significant political role, but he could not for long keep himself away from controversy. In 1665 Dr. Nedham returned to battle in a new arena. Specifically he was challenging the current medical establishment, but in a larger sense he was siding with the Moderns against the Ancients. His weapon, a 500-page book, was licensed in September 1664 and published a few months later. Its full title flings down the gauntlet:

Medala Medicinae

A Plea

For the Free Profession, and a Renovation of the Art of Physick Out of the Noblest and most Authentick Writers.

	(The Publick Advantages of its Liberty.

Shewing
    (The Publick Advantages of its Liberty.
    (The Disadvantage that comes to the
    (Publick by any sort of Physicians,
    (imposing upon the Studies and
    (Practise of others.
    (The Alteration of Diseases from their
    (old State and Condition.
    (The Causes of that Alteration.
    (The Insufficiency and Uselessness of
    (meer Scholastick Methods and
    (Medicines, with a necessity of new.

Tending to the Rescue of Mankind from the Tyranny of Diseases; and of Physicians themselves, from the Pedantisim of Old Authors and present Dictators.

The Author, M.N. Med. Londineus.

    Medice, Cura Teipsum.

    <u>Medala Medicinae</u> is a readable work, but confusing to me, the wrong kind of doctor. In discussing it I therefore rely heavily on Lester King's <u>The Road to Medical Enlightenment, 1650-1695</u>,[12] supplemented by certain background information in Christoper Hill's <u>Change and Continuity in Seventeenth-century England</u>. Nedham is more self-reliant than I. In the Dedication he announced "that from his youth [he] hath been conversant in the Studies of Physick, and came young to the practise of it in this great City, above twenty years ago."

    The book is a massive argument in favor of the iatrochemists—those, that is, who use chemical remedies—and against the traditionalists, who stick with Galenic medicine.[13] Consequently it supports the amateur doctor against the professional, the experimentalist against the established practitioner, the man dirtied by working in his own laboratory against the man in the clean white coat. Just as Milton had said that every man could be his own minister, and as the Levellers had said that every man could be his own lawyer, so Nedham was saying, if somewhat indirectly, that every man could be his own doctor.

William Walwyn, the most sophisticated spokesman for Leveller doctrines, became an iatrochemical physician after the collapse of his cause in 1649. Samuel Hartlib, the prestigious advocate of educational reform, supported iatrochemistry.[14] And under the leadership of Franciscus de le Boe Sylvius, the medical faculty at Leyden between 1658 and 1672 was the center for the teaching and preaching of iatrochemical medicine.[15]

Specifically, <u>Medala Medicinae</u> attacks the College of Physicians. In the process Nedham defends those doctors with less formal training, like himself, and the growing number of semi-professional apothecaries and surgeons in England. As an experienced propagandist he of course took the offensive. Since the medical establishment, and especially the College of Physicians, relied on tradition, he tried to overthrow that tradition. In the words of Lester King, <u>Medala Medicinae</u> is "a work of special pleading and not at all of original observation. Nedham occasionally referred to patients he himself had treated, but these references are few and play no significant part in his argument. The book is a congeries of quotations, assertions, arguments, inferences, refutations, and logic-chopping."[16] Here is one of hundreds of examples in the book that can validate King's description: It is the "interest of the collegiate Corporations of Physitians...not to permit a new laborious sect of Philospophers, working Knowledg out of the Fire, by their Industry and Successes, to bring a reproach upon them for their Idleness."[17]

To support his argument Nedham claims that there have been major recent alterations in certain diseases; hence the traditonalists are out-of-date: "He is but a dull Practiser that doth not yearly see Agues and Fevers appearing in new forms."[18] As illustrations of this he stresses syphilis and scurvy, two relatively new diseases which have joined to change "the whole Frame of Nature in Mankind, and all the diseases thereto belonging."[19] It is therefore foolish to use treatments that were popular twenty or thirty years ago; only new remedies can diminish "the number of those little Innocents which are yearly snatch'd away by an untimely death."[20] King's summary of Nedham's hypothesis is less sentimental:

> Diseases have changed their character. Pox and scurvy are universal diseases; they may appear under their own nature or may simulate other diseases or, by participation, may complicate all other diseases. Since pox and scurvy are transmitted from parent to child (as well as from one sexual partner to another) they are inescapable. Old remedies do not help, and consequently new remedies are necessary. The College of Physicians is the bastion of the old remedies, while the chemists are those who provide new remedies.[21]

Nedham demonstrates that he was aware of the discoveries which the new microscopists were making and that he had studied the works of Robert Boyle.[22] Consequently he had developed an interest in organisms too small to be seen by the naked eye, generally called "animalculae," though he usually refers to them as "worms." Starting in 1660 he prescribed vermifuges to kill them. He became convinced that juleps and other "chemical" worm-killers would be beneficial in all diseases, and that no disease could be cured until the "worms" had been eliminated.[23] "The Insufficiency and Uselessness of the old Way of Physick, in respect of Method and Medicines... [proves] a necessity of a new."[24] The "empirics" therefore should have, indeed must have, full liberty to practise.

King sumamrizes his account of Nedham with the paradoxical statement that he is a "splendid example of correct conclusions and incorrect premises....On the basis of bad logic and neglect of scientific attitude, he nevertheless propounded conclusions which the course of time has justified....Lacking in critical judgement, [he] helped to bring about a critical attitude in his opponents."[25] King may be correct about the long run, but the iatrochemical movement quickly attracted a variety of quacks, astrologers, magicians, and the seventeenth-century equivalent of patent medicine salesmen. The College of Physicians of course utilized this to smear the movement and, despite the example of Boyle and his well-trained colleagues, chemistry--and iatrochemistry--languished for the next century.[26]

Medala Medicinae elicited four rebuttals, of which the most impressive is John Twysden's Medicina Veterum, published in 1666. It is a lengthy point-by-point refutation of Nedham which is defensive, tradition-bound, and not very convincing.[27] In 1667 George Castle in The Chymical Galenist took up the establishment cudgels, but with similar lack of effectiveness. Both he and Twysden used ad hominem arguments. Castle, for instance, calls Nedham "this bold and impertinent invader of Physick," having previously designated him as a man "whose business and profession it has been for above twenty years, to libel all sacred and honourable persons of this Nation."[28]

Nedham in 1674 thus disposed of the "four champions" who had answered Medala Medicinae:

> I shall let their Names die with themselves; Two of them are gone already; the third (I hear) is often buried in Ale at a place called The Hole in the Wall; and the Fourth hath asked me pardon before Company, confessing that he was set up by the Brotherhood of the Confederacy [the College of Physicians].[29]

In May 1665, from his house in the "Thomas Apostles" section of London, Nedham contributed a Preface to Edward Bolnest's Medicina Instaurata. Bolnest, a physician, also vigorously preached the iatrochemical approach, and his title-page announces that the author of Medala Medicinae is contributing to this book. Nedham echoes Bolnest's flattering dedication to the Duke of Buckingham, "whether you take him in the Chymical, or in his Politick capacity," and bestows a similar double compliment on Bolnest: "that men may know how learned and judiciously you write, as well as operate." In his Preface he repeats the substance of his attacks on the traditionalists and of his support of the hypotheses advanced in Medala Medicinae. At one point he almost sings his Baconianism:

> We who profess Chymical Principles and Operations are never better pleased, than when we hear of numbers of Professors and Operators coming in to us, because we know the Harvest is great, and the true Labourers few; there are in the field of Nature, yet undiscovered, Secrets enough for Ages to fetch forth, and to find work for all the world....

And he goes on to advocate the erection of a large number of experimental medical laboratories.

In explaining why he has "no cause to repent" of anything he wrote in Medala Medicinae, Nedham defends himself and his colleagues against the establishment charge that the iatrochemists are a bunch of proletarian quacks by displaying his own elitist connections. He refers to an "Audience at the King's Council-Table" for him and his medical associates, at which "with...Princely Grace an ear was given to every man of us." Moreover, his book has found "a general acceptance in the land, especially among the Nobler and the Learneder part."

Nedham's third and last printed contribution to medical controversy was a nineteen-page Preface to Franciscus De Le Boë, Sylvius, A New Idea Of The Practise of Physic, originally written in 1671 and published in an English translation in 1675. Again Nedham defends chemical medicine, but strangely enough he opposes autopsies. He eulogizes Sylvius in a short biography, and argues for a "Reformation" of medical education so that "our Youth for Physick, instead of Academics, be brought up more Mechanico."[30] But more relevant to this study are his personal touches. He admits that in <u>Medala Medicinae</u> he "chose rather to cloth myself with Quotations from Head to Foot, borrowed out of the Writings of the most Learned Men in the World, to render myself as invincible as might be." He brags that during the ten years since then he has not altered his medical theories or practice, except in one respect:

> No man hath at all times, made more constant use of Animals and Vegetables in his Practice than I have done, as my Bills at the Apothecaries will shew. Some years ago, there was a more ready Opportunity to scandalise me, when my matter of Medicine being prepared in my own House was kept private to my self, and so my Adversaries might maliciously say of it what they would: Therefore, as soon as I found the Company of Apothecaries had erected a Laboratory at their Hall, for supply of their Shops with Medicins of all sorts, of the Chymical Preparation...my Heart rose with pleasure... [at] an Undertaking so necessary for the Kingdom.

Regardless of what he had brewed or the apothecaries packaged, he announces that he has "a purpose to publish some Essays of my own, to discover what may be done by more able Men, towards an advancement of Knowledg in the Powers of Plants."

But during the final two years of his life, in his writing though not in his vocation, Nedham turned away from plants and returned to politics. Shortly before, in February 1676, he was almost certainly the Dr. Needham who was the recipient of a ₤50 bequest when the will of Sir Peter Wentworth cleared probate. Wentworth, who had been a cantakerous member of the Long Parliament and of Cromwell's Council of State, probably left him this money as a friend, not as a patient. He also bequeathed ₤100 to John Milton, though Milton died before he could inherit it.[31]

Nedham vigorously survived until November 1678, and in five controversial pamphlets he re-entered the national arena as a paid propagandist for Charles II. No essayist on the Powers of Plants, as well as no Miltonic Samson Agonistes, Nedham made his last exit as a full-fledged Tory.

The first of these pamphlets appeared late in 1676: <u>A Pacquet of Advice and Animadversions, Sent from London To the Men of Shaftesbury.... Occasioned by a Seditious Pamphlet, Intituled, A Letter from a Person of Quality to His Friend in the Country</u>. Nedham was back on the government payroll and back in politics, this time quite literally in party politics. The faction he was supporting was the incipient Tory Party, its opposition the incipient Whigs. Yet he no doubt felt right at home, and his manner of getting the job of royal propagandist has a distinctly déjà vu quality.

In 1682, after the last of the judicial murders resulting from the Popish Plot had been perpetrated, Robert Ferguson, in <u>The Third Part of No Protestant Plot</u>, claimed that a corrupt judge had introduced Nedham to the Earl of Danby in order to set up Nedham's defamation of Shaftesbury. Danby was Charles's skilled and aggressive Lord Treasurer; Shaftesbury was the leader of the opposition to the King. <u>A Pacquet of Advice</u> and its sequel, <u>A Second Pacquet of Advice</u>, were written, says Ferguson, "according to his [Nedham's] wonted method of treating all he wrote against; he loads this Honourable Person [Shaftesbury] with all the Aspersions his Wit, influenced by the Malice and Revenge of others, could invent and suggest." Ferguson then cites a letter from the judge to Nedham suggesting that he get in touch with Danby.[32] What thickens the plot and adds to the déjà vu quality is that the judge, Edmund Warcup, was a conspiratorial type who frequently changed and muddied his allegiances; indeed, he weaves in and out of Shaftesbury's life in a snaky pattern.[33] But like Bradshaw and Lenthall a quarter of a century earlier, Danby made a good bargain.

Regardless of how much he paid Nedham--and it is probable that he promised him Ł500 and actually paid him Ł50[34]--Danby assisted him by suppressing some, though by no means all, pro-Shaftesbury pamphlets. Further, he saw that both <u>Pacquets</u> were widely circulated and that the first was promptly republished. Danby delegated these arrangements to his chief censor, Sir Roger L'Estrange, the government's leading journalist in the 1660's, and thus in many ways Nedham's successor.[35] Appropriately, <u>A Pacquet of Advice</u> emphasizes the parallels between 1641 and 1676. Now, however, Nedham was a staunch supporter of King and bishops, an opponent of calling a new--and potentially Whig--Parliament. Now he can remind his readers:

> Therefore neither Cavaliers nor Churchmen can, after so late and sad an experience of Alterability and Alteration, be such fools as not to understand what they have seen and felt, by such alternative humors as are now afloat again; and what the Issue of them would be if they [the men of Shaftesbury] might have way: especially seeing the same Presbyterian Faction are brewing afresh.

Most of the seventy-four pages of <u>A Pacquet</u> are given over to a caustic attack on Shaftesbury and an ad hominem refutation of <u>A Letter from a Person of Quality</u>, as if the letter had been written by Shaftesbury. Nedham has the gall to call him a changeling, a man prepared to "shift principles like shirts." Yet Nedham, his brother under the skin, did not pull his punches. He describes the Earl as "Mephistopheles, the Fairy Fiend that haunts both Houses; of whom I have been told, the witty Duke of Buckingham likened him to a Will-with-a-Wisp, that uses to lead men out of the way; then leaves them at last in a ditch and darkness, and nimbly retreats for self-security." Or, equally sardonic and belittling: "Now (I suppose) he hath lived to see the utmost of his old trade of juggling, having juggled himself out of all at court, and having past hope of juggling himself in again (all his feats being well understood there ---) he sets up at t'other end o' the town to juggle up a mutiny in the City; in hope to find combustible matter thus to set fire to in the country." Shaftesbury is not only a will-of-the-wisp and a juggler, he is also a political deadbeat: "It is at this time a great question among his Friends in the City, Whether they shall take security upon his Lordships Honour....For Silk, or Cloth, or Stuffs, or the like, they are ready enough to give him Credit, but if ye talk of State-Commodities, they shrink their shoulders, and say nothing."

Shaftesbury's modern biographer, K.H.D. Haley, acknowledges the effectiveness of A Pacquet of Advice:

> It was a powerful indictment; it was set out in pithy, quotable, colloquial language; it was all good fun [shades of John Berkenhead]; it rested on the fact that Shaftesbury had for thirteen years been a member of the government which he was now opposing; and it appealed to the perpetual readiness of the man in the street to believe that a politician who changes his affiliations must do so for dishonest or ambitious reasons and cannot possess any inner consistency....Shaftesbury agents were portrayed as here, there and everywhere, ready to revive the Old Faction of Forty-One, and even to use the dreadful arguments of John Lilburne against a Long Parliament.[36]

Parliament had been prorogued in December 1675 and it reconvened in February 1677. Shortly thereafter Shaftesbury was committed to the Tower. Haley credits--or debits--the failure of Shaftesbury and his followers mainly to A Pacquet of Advice, and he quotes an anonymous source that, "Out of twenty peers who had been in a firm league [with Shaftesbury]...sixteen dropped off upon perusal and well digestion of that book."[37]

A Second Pacquet of Advice and Animadversions Sent to the Men of Shaftesbury is very like its predecessor. It was published in May 1677, "Occasioned by several seditious Pamphlets Spread abroad to pervert the People, since the publication of the Former Pacquet." Most of its seventy-six pages are in rebuttal to four pro-Shaftesbury pamphlets which had slipped past L'Estrange.[38] Again Nedham staunchly supports the King and the Established Church, and again he views with alarm the ostensible parallel between Interregnum radicals and 1677 Whigs. "'Tis very fine (ye men of Shaftesbury) this is so like the language of the old Levellers, who were all for ruling by turns." The author of *The Excellencie Of A Free State* even quotes with approval Charles I's rejection of the moderate Propositions tendered him by Parliament in 1642. Nedham appears to be horrorstruck by the Whigs' desire for "a Switzerland Reformation" and by their employment of "Popular Uproar" to attain their divisive ends. Adroitly he links fear of the past to fear of the future:

> ...If the same Opinions and Principles that brought on the First war be now again abroach, have we not cause to believe they meant, or may mean, a Second? If the same Faction be at work again that contrived the First War, and they as severe with the King as they were with his Father in disputing his Royalty, seminating Fears and Jealousies among the People, and new trimming the old Bridle and Saddle of Presbytery to run down the Bishops, circumcise the Crown, set Christ in the Throne (as they ever most Hypocritically pretended, to the shame of Christianity) thereby to ride King and Lords and out-rant the Kingdom: If these things were designed and transacted, the Party form'd and ready instructed by Pamphlets spread in Citie and Country, and their hearts full of hope before the Session of Parliament in February last to have accomplished their work, shall we yet doubt of their Intent because they did not effect it? There is reason enough to inform our understanding: that they

gave us the Premises, though they could not the Conclusion.

An extant letter from a Londoner to a friend in the country, written in July, testifies that A Second Pacquet was also effective:

> The first part of the Answer to the men of Shaftesbury our old friend March Needham is reported to have a finger in, and in the second Answer a hand, and also a piece called the Countermine is said to be his, at which our Nonconforming friends are much troubled, saying that this piece is the most inveterate that ever was writ against them, yet they seem to favour the second Answer to the men of Shaftesbury that seems to answer all the papers about the esse of the P[arliament], especially that part about the words "If he shall see cause to call a Parliament oftener than once a year" in the Statute of Edward III. 'Tis said these three papers will be answered.[39]

The third of Nedham's Tory tracts is clever and nasty. Early in the spring of 1678 he published Honesty's best Policy, Or, Penitence the Sum of Prudence: Being a briefe Discourse in honour of Shaftesbury's Acknowledgement and Submission. Much of it is, as the title suggests, a sustained gloat--a genre in which Nedham had some experience. On February 25 Shaftesbury made a full apology for his past indiscretions, and two days later he resumed his seat in the House of Lords. Danby was mortified, and presumably he retained Nedham to squeeze whatever pro-government propaganda he could out of Shaftesbury's repentance.[40] Nedham squeezed hard.

Claiming it was "a charitable public-good work" to publicize Shaftesbury's recantation, Nedham printed in full the Earl's recent "humble petitions" and the apologetic speech he delivered on February 25. He uses the remainder of his eighteen pages to attack Shaftesbury, in the manner of both Pacquets, for having been a malcontent. Nedham works up a special anger at his having instituted an "office of intelligence to coin news for the coffee-houses; and an academy for inventing seditious and treasonable pamphlets, with directions how to print and spread them, to edify both City and kingdom into an oblivion of their allegiance." Repeatedly Nedham accentuates Shaftesbury's "Machiavellianism" by citing his words and by calling attention to "the peaceful condition of this kingdom...before...Shaftesbury began to offend." In passing, Nedham criticizes Andrew Marvell for supporting the Earl and for worrying about Popery.

Marvell's worries were justified. Since 1670 Charles had been accepting money under the table from Louis XIV and simultaneously pretending to threaten war against France. In February 1678 Louis temporarily stopped his payments, and Charles summoned Parliament to raise money for a war against the French. England, however, did not go to war; and in the summer Louis signed a peace treaty, largely on his own terms, with the Dutch, at the same time paying Charles another secret subsidy. The proroguing of Parliament in July added to the mounting anti-French sentiments, now being fanned by the Whigs for partisan reasons, by the London establishment for economic reasons, and by the urban street crowds for anti-Catholic reasons. This is the broad background for Nedham's penultimate tract, published probably in midsummer 1678: The Pacquet-Boat Advice: Or A Discourse Concerning the War with France. In it he had to walk a tightrope between supporting the current shaky peace or promoting an immediate war. At the moment there was no overt official partyline, though Danby was anti-French and during the previous year he had worked hard to arrange the marriage of the Duke of York's eldest daughter, Mary, to William of Orange. Nedham, in his balancing act, tilts toward the militants, and in so doing he shows some talent as an incipient novelist. The Pacquet-Boat Advice has the format of Dryden's An Essay of Dramatic Poesy, but Nedham adds a dash of Aphra Behn.

The three speakers in the Discourse are himself as moderator, though with an anti-French bias; a blunt chauvinistic English captain; and a suave, slippery, hypocritical French merchant. The setting is the deck of a Calais-Dover boat, then an inn in Dover. The message of this twenty-one-page pamphlet is fuzzy. Nedham ends up advocating either war with France or an "honourable peace" which would maintain the balance of power. But his characterizations and his comments as moderator are hawkish: if not war, at least the threat of war is necessary to keep France in her place. The following four quotations can convey this basically aggressive stance and, at the same time, suggest Nedham's potential talent as a writer of fiction.

First, Nedham as moderator:

This Jealousie, that he [the French Merchant] did trade with these great persons only for Diamonds, having once infected my imagination, I had a curiosity to drive it as far as I could, with all the studied Ignorance and Simplicity I was capable of, and pretending great kindness to this Nation, a folly too common and usually true with the English, who are wont with a kind of Witchcraft to dote upon the French. So that we fell smartly upon the Subject of War, and in regard I appear'd most forward in my Civility, and ready to entertain his discourse, he thought he had met with a right English Spaniel.

Next, two short speeches by the English captain:

Sir, said the Gentleman, raising himself a little, I know not whether we can part with our money, but we will part with our blood freely, 'tis said indeed you part with yours, and shoot golden Bullets, and make use of Keys of the same metal, which will open a breach or a Gate into the strongest Fortifications; but Sir we have been used to do it with Steel and

159

Iron, and yet give me leave to tell you, I hope we shall be so wise, rather to part with our money, than to keep it till the French comes with arm'd Troops to collect it, as they do in their own Country, and I hope, yet before I die to help to open some of the Gates of Paris with that hard metal, and to hear the drums beat the heavy English march through the Streets again, which once spoil'd a Jest of one of your Kings.

And:

What cryed the Captain, the French without designs? you shall as soon find a Monkey without tricks: From the Onyon Porridge-man to the Mareschal you are all Politicians and designers. You have, you say, an hundred Sail of Ships, and two hundred thousand Men, and you have no designs nor ever had I warrant you to make yourselves Masters of Flanders, Germany, Holland, and England at last.

Finally, the concluding paragraphs of **The Pacquet-Boat Advice**:

Come Captain, said I, Unity, Secrecy, and Expedition added to our Courage, and Power, may do much, and I doubt not, but the necessity which seems to be upon us will make them all meet; the Cause is good for it is not for Soveraignity, but for Safety, not for Glory but Security, and to preserve the Protestant Religion, our Lives, Liberties, and Estates, from the Rapine and Ambition of the French, and he is no true Englishman who will not heartily venture his Life and Fortune, in such a lawful War.

Upon which, Supper came in, and we having talk'd ourselves into a good opinion of eating, we gratifi'd our Pallates as well as the place would afford, and not long after every one retir'd to his Appartment, where I believe the Captain dream't of Drums, and Trumpets, and Cannons, and Granado's Storms, and Battels, for he made a horrible noise in his sleep lying in the next Room to me, for my part, like a person not much concern'd I slept, as heartily as the Souldier would permit me, who gave me several Alarms; and I can no more tell, what I dream't, than I can tell certainly what all men long so much to know, that we shall have a War with France, or such a Peace as shall be Safe and Honourable for England and all Christendome.

War with France did not occur, Danby was impeached at the end of 1678, and early in 1679 the Long Parliament of the Restoration was finally dissolved.[41] Nedham did not live long enough to develop his talents as a novelist. His final political pamphlet appeared shortly before his death in November 1678: <u>Christianissimus Christianandus. Or, Reason for the Reduction of France To a More Christian State in Europ</u>. It was promptly translated and reprinted in both Germany and France.[42] Nedham would no doubt have been gratified that the title of the German edition refers to him as "Eines Englischen Patrioten." He might have been surprised that it was republished in France, for this eighty-page tract is a vigorous call for war against the French, war right now.

<u>Christianissimus Christianandus</u> is a fitting finale to Nedham's long career as a propagandist in its stylistic variety, its range of historical allusions, and its polemical shrewdness. He begins by equating the French with the Turks in a manner that is at once condescending and alarmist:

> Certainly tis high time to think of making the Ministers of France better Christians.... Absolute power at home, and Universal Empire Abroad, is their Aim as well as the Turks.... For though France be the owner of the better Faith, yet the other keep the Faith better, because all Travellers tell us that the Turk counts it Religion to keep Word and Promise.[43]

He then elaborates, with many examples, on the propensity of the French for war, their Machiavellian diplomacy, and their ever more threatening megalomania. They have followed "Old Nicholas the Florentine [who] saith, Rattles were invented to please Children, and Oaths men: That is to say, to make men meer children."[44] Nedham's case that, as the French "have observed no Rule of Justice in making War, so they have had little regard to it in observing Peace," is well constructed and well supported.[45] He concludes with a call for a "Joynt War" against France, answers the objections, and ends up "proving" that a just war is better than an unjust peace.

In the course of his militant argument Nedham praises the aging Prince Rupert, once the dashing leader of Charles I's cavalry. With much documentation, he also analyzes French intrigues with the Scottish Presbyterians going back to 1639. Recurrently he depicts the French as anti-Christian: "Peace was the subject of Christ's last Sermon; the great Legacy that he bequeathed to his Followers. What Christians then are they, that make it their Interest and Business to destroy it on Earth!"[46] Perhaps Nedham's deftest touch is when he mocks his countrymen in order to heighten their anti-French feelings:

> While we (such is the fondness of our Nation!) are bewitched with an affectation of French Commodities, though but meer Baubles and Gugaws, and though our own Workmen afterwards work better and out-do them in the making of their own Inventions yet (such is our base folly!) unless the Retailers of them do swear, and lie too, that they are French-made, there's no putting them off to advantage at a quick rate. Moreover, we must have all French about us; their Behaviour, their Fashions, their Garb...their mean way of House-keeping....French musick, French Dancing-Masters, French Air in our very Countenances, French Legs, French Hats, French Compliments, French Grimaces; only we have not so frequent

the French shrug of the shoulder, because we are not generally so low---and itchy.[47]

Nedham's own final shrug of the shoulders--or final insertion of his tongue in his cheek--may be his sneer at aggressive, controversial journalists near the end of <u>Christianissimus Christianandus</u>:

> If the Parliament chance at any time to be Prorogued or Adjourn'd, that Season proves to this sort of News-mongers, like a nipping Frost to Flies, and they are ever ready to die away like fainting Grasshoppers. There's nothing revives them in the Interval, like some unlucky Mischief befal'n the Court. Tis Mischief they gape for; and yet are but Fools at doing it, and therefore ought to be better instructed.[48]

Nedham did not need to be better instructed, nor did he have time. In Wood's words, "At length this most seditious, mutable and railing author... died suddenly in the house of one Kidder in D'eureux Court near Temple-bar London...and was buried on the 19th of Novemb...at the upper end of the body of the church of St. Clement's Danes, near the entrance into the chancel."[49] Two years later, when the chancel was rebuilt, Nedham's monument, such as it may have been, was removed or defaced.[50]

Probably his death was sudden, for he died intestate--but not in poverty. In December 1678 an administrator was appointed to settle Nedham's estate, an estate large enough for that administrator to have to post a bond.[51] Since then Nedham's ghost has flitted sporadically across the pages of commentators and historians, a protean and sinister minor shadow.

Chapter V Footnotes

1. Quoted in Muddiman, King's Journalist, pp. 111f.

2. Wood, p. 1182. Masson, Milton, VI, 202, says that Wood hints that Hyde was the man Nedham bribed, and adds that the suggestion is "preposterous." I agree.

3. Quoted in Masson, Milton, VI, 200.

4. G.N. Clark, The Later Stuarts 1660-1714, Oxford: At the Clarendon Press, 1947, p. 56.

5. Wood, pp. 1182f.

6. I am assuming that A Short History first appeared in the spring of 1661. Some time that year a second edition, "Corrected and Amended," was published as part of a 94-page book, following The True Character Of a Rigid Presbyter: With a Narrative of the Dangerous Designes of the English and Scottish Covenanters. 'To the Reader' is signed "Mercurius Pragmaticus," but I am certain that only The Short History is by Nedham. (See also Brian Morris and Eleanor Withington, eds., The Poems of John Cleveland, Oxford: At the Clarendon Press, 1967, p. 138: the statement that Nedham disowned The True Character.) Cleveland in the mid 1640's wrote at least part of this "Character," almost certainly including the two pages (31f.) which are most incisive and Overburyan. Later in 1661 an edition consisting only of The True Character appeared, and this was reissued in 1711.

7. The first 112 stanzas are from nos. 1 to 28 of Mercurius Pragmaticus; then, without a gap, come the title-page poems from nos. 1 to 38 of a new series of Pragmaticus, but

7. (cont.) skipping nos. 17 and 26, which apparently were not edited by Nedham.

8. Wood, p. 1187.

9. Parker, *Milton*, pp. 1102, 1387.

10. Masson, *Milton*, VI, 452. Hill, *Milton*, p. 214, suggests that after 1660 the relationship between Milton and Nedham "soon again had political overtones," as their names were linked together in at least four hostile pamphlets.

11. It is possible that Nedham had long been interested in educational reform. A cryptic note written by Samuel Hartlib in 1647 mentions "Needham" as one of the possible "Commissioners for the Act of the Council for schooling" (Parker, *Milton*, p. 312). *A Discourse* (p. 13) has a reference to Nedham's own children, but as far as I can ascertain, he had only one child: a son, Marchamont, born to his first wife, Lucy, in May 1652 (Firth *DNB*).

12. Lester King, *The Road to Medical Enlightenment, 1650-1695*, London: Macdonald, 1970.

13. For the general medical background of this controversy, see Inglis, *History of Medicine*, pp. 104ff.

14. Hill, *Change and Continuity*, pp. 168-174.

15. C.D. O'Malley, ed., *The History of Medical Education*, Berkeley: University of California Press, 1970, p. 204: from the chapter by G.A. Lindeboom, "Medical Education in the Netherlands 1575-1750." On p. 233 of *Medala Medicinae* Nedham quotes Sylvius to support his own position.

16. King, *Road to Medical Enlightenment*, p. 148.

17. *Medala Medicinae*, p. 8.

18. *Medala Medicinae*, p. 33.

19. *Medala Medicinae*, pp. 40f.

20. *Medala Medicinae*, p. 46.

21. King, *Road to Medical Enlightenment*, p. 148.

22. *Medala Medicinae*, e.g., pp. 215ff., 503.

23. King, *Road to Medical Enlightenment*, pp. 151-153.

24. This quotation is the title of Chapter 6 in *Medala Medicinae*.

25. King, *Road to Medical Enlightenment*, p. 154.

26. Hill, *Change and Continuity*, p. 175.

27. It is summarized in King, *Road to Medical Enlightenment*, pp. 154-156.

28. Castle, *Chymical Galenist*, the "Epistle Dedicatory." Another rebuttal, which I have not seen, is Robert Sprackling, *Medala Ignorantiae*. I do not know the name of the fourth serious rebuttal.

29. From Nedham's prefatory 'To the Reader,' in Franciscus De Le Boe, Sylvius, *A New Idea Of The Practise of Physic*. London, 1675. (Nedham's Preface was written in 1674.)

30. Wood, p. 1189, seems almost pleased with Nedham's derogation of university degrees, and devotes eight lines to quotations from Nedham's attack on traditional medical education.

31. French, *Life Records*, V. 64. For Wentworth, see the biography by Firth in *DNB*.

32. Robert Ferguson, The Third Part of No Protestant Plot, London, 1682, p. 586. See Wood, p. 1188, who also connects Warcup and Danby with Nedham.

33. See K. H. D. Haley, The First Earl of Shaftesbury, Oxford: Clarendon Press, 1968, passim. Ferguson in No Protestant Plot, London, 1681, includes a lengthy attack on Warcup, along with refutations of Nedham--but without naming him.

34. Firth, DNB.

35. For a brief account of L'Estrange's journalistic career, see Wood, under Nedhjam, p. 1185. At the time of the Restoration L'Estrange had attacked Nedham, the first instance probably being in L'Estrange His Apology. (see French, Life Records, IV, 299.)

36. Haley, Shaftesbury, p. 414.

37. Haley, Shaftesbury, p. 415.

38. Some Considerations upon the Question, Whether the Parliament is dissolved by its Prorogation; The Long Parliament Dissolved; A Seasonable Question and an Useful Answer; A Narrative of the cause and manner of the Imprisonment of the Lords, now close Prisoners in the Tower of London.

39. Calendar of State Papers, Domestic, 1677-78, p. 226. For the answers to Nedham, see Haley, Shaftesbury, pp. 659-661. I have been unable to trace "the Countermine," and I can find no other reference to it in connection with Nedham. Dryden's 'Absalom and Achitophel' is of course the most famous product of this anti-Shaftesbury campaign.

40. Haley, Shaftesbury, pp. 438-441.

41. To wind up the story of Shaftesbury: he flourished politically until 1682, when he was barely acquitted of a charge of treason. He then fled to Holland, where early in 1683 he died.

42. <u>Christianissimus Christianandus, Oder Eines Englischen Patrioten Wolgegrundete Beweg-Urascher Durch was Mittel Frankreich zueinem Christlichen Stande zu bewegen</u>, no Place, 1678; <u>Christianissimus Christianandus, Ou Le Moyen de Reduire La France A Un Etat plus Chrestien Pour le bien de l'Europe</u>, no place or date, but I would guess Paris and early 1679.

43. <u>Christianissimus</u>, p. 3.

44. <u>Christianissimus</u>, p. 18.

45. <u>Christianissimus</u>, p. 17.

46. <u>Christianissimus</u>, p. 60.

47. <u>Christianissimus</u>, pp. 36f.

48. <u>Christianissimus</u>, pp. 73f.

49. Wood, p. 1189.

50. Firth, <u>DNB</u>.

51. Public Record Office: Probate 6/53, folio 119 L.H.

CHAPTER VI
CODA

Nedham died as the Polish Plot was escalating into its two-year run as an ugly tragi-farce. I like to think he would have tried to mitigate its excesses: he had been working for Charles II, and he would have found such characters as Titus Oates tempting targets. Also--and this is more conjectural--he would have viewed this outbreak of murderous McCarthyism as politically and philosophically repugnant. But are there any more relative grounds to catch the conscience of a turncoat?

In describing his four major turns--his movements--I have tried to depict him objectively, warts and all. Perhaps on occasion I have overemphasized the blemishes and not given him the benefit of a few cosmetic patches. On the other hand, I have usually tried to select quotations from him which display his stylistic variety and wit, as well as depict his stance at any particular moment. But I have postponed any over-all judgment of the man. What follows, therefore, is intended to be a sort of moral denouement, combined with a touch of revisionist history.

My original title for this book was 'The Nine Lives of Marchamont Nedham.' I first toyed with the idea of getting to nine by dividing his political spectrum into segments ranging from Harringtonian republicanism to High-Church Toryism. But this did not work: the spectral bands shifted, blurred, overlapped. More functional was a vocational breakdown: Teacher, Law Clerk, Journalist, Pamphleteeer, Doctor, Spy, Press Agent, Versifier, Political Theorist. The total is nine, but the last two are not really vocations in terms of Nedham's life; nor can "Friend of Milton," a category I wanted to include, be considered a job. So I settled for <u>Cromwell's Press Agent</u>, which does, after all, suggest the high point and chronological center of Nedham's career. Certainly he was many-faceted.

Every commentator on him, from 1645 to today, has accused him of being at least two-faced. Masson gives him an occasional good word. Knachel and Pocock speak well of his contributions as a political theorist, and King praises his role in the history of medicine. His contemporaries, among them Wood, pay reluctant tribute to Nedham's wit and verbal dexterity. Since then most of the small number of historians who bother to mention him repeat this faint praise. But for more than three centuries all have agreed that he was an unprincipled turncoat, motivated by greed and self-interest: a venal and often vicious Vicar of Bray.

Their case is strong. Nedham first supported Parliament and army against the King. Next he became a prominent and strident Royalist. Then he served as the chief editor and publicist for the Commonwealth and Protectorate. He ended his career as a High-Church Tory propagandist for Charles II. It is thus at once a professional compliment and a moral insult to him that Charles I, Cromwell, and Charles II each forgave him his past sins in order to secure his services. And Nedham made sure that he was well paid or otherwise rewarded for these services. Thus his is certainly a success story in terms of money and power, though as a seventeenth-century Horatio Alger he is by no means an exemplar of the Puritan ethic.

Their case is strong but not watertight. Nedham could plead guilty, then ask for a light sentence from posterity because of his contributions to English sub-literature. Such a tactic might appeal to his sense of humor. I have already quoted his praise of Thomas More's "jocoserio style, betwixt jest and earnest," and his comment that when More lost his knack for "drolling" and became too serious, he got his head chopped off. Nedham kept his head and managed to contribute to the polemical literature of the Interregnum a rare and recurrent touch of humor. Often it was his "drollery," his mockery and irreverence, that infuriated his opponents more than the substance of what he wrote. From his attacks on Berkenhead to his denigration of Shaftesbury he displayed his mastery of the joco-serio style. For what is is worth, I find him the most readable polemicist of the mid-seventeenth century.[1] Certainly he was influential to the extent that his opponents of all stripes tried to answer him in kind.

His second contribution to English subliterature was what he did for journalism. More than any of his competitors he made the weekly newspaper professional.[2] He was skilled in gathering, condensing, and clarifying the news; he employed a wide variety of styles; and his serious editorials were unmatched. Yet his contribution was relatively short-lived: a semi-free press died with the Restoration and did not fully revive for almost a century.

Third, as a satiric poet Nedham at his best is Dryden's equal. At his normal level he is a little better than most of his contemporary popular versifiers, with the exception of John Cleveland. Fourth, his contribution to the literature of political theory lies in the liveliness and assortment of his styles. His ideas he derived from others. Finally, his written contribution to medicine is similar, for in this area too he was a popularizer rather than an orginal thinker.

Nedham would, I think, agree with this assessment. He often publicly boasted of his humor, his competence as an editor, his ability to handle a variety of rhetorical modes, and his skill in reaching a wide audience. He did not publicly boast of the fact that in all his literary roles he made money. Even his attacks on the medical establishment probably paid off in the form of more patients, attracted to Dr. Nedham by the attendant publicity. As journalist, pamphleteer, and press agent he was unquestionably the most highly paid of any of his colleagues. His direct paymaster was usually someone from the highest inner circle of government, whether Essex or Charles I or Cromwell or Thurloe or Danby. But his audience was the broad outer circle, the general public. In his fifteen years as a journalist, and especially during the 1650's, he had the largest cumulative readership of any writer, even including the astrologers. Presumably he influenced that audience by both informing and goading it. I am convinced by my own research in Interregnum sub-literature that the average male Londoner in 1660 was more literate and more politically aware than his counterpart of twenty years earlier. It is in this amorphous area that Nedham's literary influence, his contribution, was greatest.

But Nedham was never a democrat, and he might reject this part of his plea, or even the entire plea of his contribution to English sub-literature. Instead, he might claim to be morally not guilty. If so, the following would be a plausible defense:

Obviously Nedham was highly intelligent and unfettered by any rigid religious or political ideology. Obviously, too, throughout much of his career he was close to those at the top of the government heap, and therefore privy to what was really going on and to what was likely to happen next. Intelligent, unfettered, well informed: why, then, was his sense of timing so bad? Why did he twice risk Thomas More's fate of getting his head chopped off by "the great politicians of this captious world"?

The first occasion on which Nedham got in trouble was when he went too far in <u>Mercurius Britanicus</u> by directly attacking and mocking the King. This instance of political prematurity can be chalked up to the exuberance of youth (Nedham was twenty-five), to lack of experience, and to the fact that a divided Parliament was not sending him clear signals. So his first stint in jail and his temporary forced departure from journalism do not indicate any firm political or philosophical stance or any disposition for danger or martyrdom.

Two years later <u>Mercurius Pragmaticus</u>, under the editorship of Nedham, became the most devastating weapon in the King's verbal armory. Yet Nedham's shift to the King is explicable on non-ideological grounds: he was bored, and the excitement and money promised by the Royalists might well have been irresistible. Moreover, in 1647 Charles was still a powerful counter in the political game. One could support him in the hope that he would side with the army against the Scots and the Presbyterians, or with what remained of the middle group in Parliament. Backing Charles at that moment did not commit a person to full-fledged Royalism; instead, in political terms, it was an open-ended gamble. Consequently some of the early numbers of <u>Pragmaticus</u> imply that the King will embrace, and be embraced by, the army. Nedham was wrong, soon 100% wrong. Yet he continued stridently to support the Royalist cause. He hung on during those months when the King's trial and conviction became predictable, then inevitable. He hung on past the King's execution, while the "Beagles of the State" searched for him and his secret press. He hung on until in June 1649 he was finally captured and sentenced to jail. Probably it was to have been a long confinement; possibly it could have meant the executioner's block. Nedham's timing, in terms of his own self-interest, could hardly have been worse.

In that autumn he signed on as a press agent for the Commonwealth. To get out of prison, to return to the excitement of politics and journalism, to be extremely well paid--these were more than adequate motives. For a decade Nedham performed his various tasks with skill and energy; politically and financially he flourished. But in the middle of this propserous period he risked his powerful position and high salary by publishing <u>The Excellencie Of A Free State</u>. In 1652 the republican ideas it espoused were not considered

173

nearly so dangerous as they were four years later when Cromwell was thinking about accepting the crown. In 1656 Harrington's Oceana, a fuller, more explicit, and better developed anticipation of the United States Constitution, was saved from being officially suppressed only by the intercession of Cromwell's daughter.[3] Though Oceana and The Excellencie share many ideas, Nedham probably felt more secure than Harrington because of his services to the Protector. Even so, his timing was at best risky.

    At the end of the decade Nedham's timing was as bad as, if not worse than, it had been ten years earlier. By late 1659 those in the know were aware that the restoration of Charles II was imminent. In the preliminary jostling and jockeying Nedham was fired and then rehired as editor of Mercurius Politicus and The Publick Intelligencer. He hung on to this position to the very end. While others were recanting or fleeing, he continued to uphold the Good Old Cause and to oppose the return of monarchy--even if his journalistic voice became increasingly muted. It was not at all muted in Newes From Brussels, which came out in March 1660, a month before the second edition of Milton's Ready and Easy Way. Both men expected to be excluded from any Royal or Parliamentary pardon. At the last minute Milton went into hiding, Nedham fled to Holland. Both were lucky and both survived. Both, in terms of self-interest, displayed terrible timing.

    Nedham's resumption of writing after the Restoration involved no risk. In the early 1660s he tried to get back into the good graces of the Royalists. His medical polemics were not personally dangerous, and his pamphlets of 1676-78 followed the government party-line, or what seemed to be that line. Nedham died of natural causes at the age of fifty-eight. But in 1648-49 and again in 1659-60 he risked long terms in prison, and certainly in the second instance his life. In between, in 1656, he jeopardized an influential and remunerative position. How do these gambles fit the portrait of a man guilty of being a venal and vicious Vicar of Bray?

Nedham was intelligent, unfettered, well informed. Whether cause or effect, he was also skeptical and pragmatic, though his skepticism often verged on cynicism, his pragmatism on expediency. He had long studied history, and he had gradually absorbed the ideas of Machiavelli and Hobbes.[4] For most of his adult life he was a skeptical pragmatist or--the same thing--a pragmatic skeptic. This was a flexible stance, an open-minded attitude, not a set theory or ideology. It can, however, be broken down into three elements. The first two generate the third, which in turn may explain Nedham's instances of bad timing, his plea of not guilty.

First, he was temperamentally and/or philosophically pragmatic and skeptical. Admittedly, he was anti-Scot, but his prejudice can be explained by the fact that it was patriotic and popular. Moreover, he usually expressed his dislike in a manner more mocking than murderous. A passage from The Case of the Commonwealth is typical: the Scots are "a people of far less generous souls, pay, and other accommodations" than the English. His dislike of the Presbyterians was more firmly grounded and more sustained. Constitutionally--in both senses of the word--he saw them as rigid, smug, intolerant: neither skeptical nor pragmatic. In terms of his own religion, though he knew the Bible well and invoked it and the name of God frequently, he was neither committed nor devout. Cumulatively his writings indicate that he was an agnostic and that he shared Hobbes's utilitarian religious views.

Second, as a diligent and responsive student of history Nedham was empirically pragmatic and skeptical. He several times pointed out that the Old Testament Jews tried many forms of government which, even with divine guidance, turned out to be a mixed bag. Classical history provided many other models of short-lived successes and failures, as did modern European history. There are no final solutions, no sure prescriptions. History always has been and always will be kaleidoscopic and unpredictable. One does one's tolerant best with the rough and unwieldy human material currently available.

This combination of philosophical and empirical skepticism-pragmatism enabled Nedham both to praise and attack such diverse groups as Catholics and Levellers, Monarchists and Republicans, army generals and London street crowds. If one made a list of those Nedham attacked and another of those he praised over a period of thirty-five years, these two lengthy lists would almost duplicate each other. This can be partly accounted for by the truism that in a revolutionary era the whirligig of time turns very quickly. It can also be partly accounted for by the third element in Nedham's skepticism-pragmatism: his fear of political, though not of rhetorical, excess.

This fear, rooted in Nedham's temperament and experience, may explain his errors in political timing. In 1648-49 it is highly possible that Nedham felt that the militants in Parliament and army were pushing the Puritan Revolution too far and too fast, that the country was heading for a military dictatorship or a Leveller-style democracy. Hence he stuck with the Royalists, the forces of tradition and reaction, to try to halt or at least delay this rush to ruin.

In 1656 when he published The Excellencie of A Free State as a book, it is highly possible that he stuck his neck out because of the same fear of political excess. The Good Old Cause then seemed headed toward a monarchy more centralized and more potent than that under James or Charles. Again Nedham did his bit to halt or at least delay this rush to ruin.

Finally, in 1659-60 he almost certainly viewed the Restoration as a massive repudiation of everything the Civil Wars had been fought for, as a return to rigidity and reaction, as well as a very real bloodbath. Again he used his pen to halt or at least delay this rush to ruin.

In each of these instances he failed--and then recanted. In each of these instances his putative pessimism turned out to be exaggerated. Yet each of these alleged predictions of his was plausible--and partly true. England in 1649 was not ready to become a republican Commonwealth. Cromwell in 1656 was a military dictator, despite his belief in civil liberties, religious toleration, and constitutional government. The Restoration did bring in its train many forms of rigidity, reaction and revenge. The country survived, even intermittently flourished. So, surprisingly, did Nedham, though he died before he had to take a stand on--and presumably against--the Popish Plot.

This book began with a reference to Arthur Koestler, so perhaps it is appropriate to conclude with him. Rubashov at the end of <u>Darkness at Noon</u> publicly refuses to denounce the cause to which he has dedicated his life, though that cause has become a hideous travesty of everything he believed in and fought for. It is possible that Nedham in 1649, and again ten years later, felt that he could not repudiate either of the two opposing causes to which he had dedicated his talents and for which he seemd willing to risk his life. But such an explanation makes him too much of an ideologue or martyr, even a potential hero. I prefer to view him as skeptical and pragmatic, sophisticated and self-aware: neither a dedicated partisan nor a vicious Vicar of Bray.

Nedham lived at a pivotal moment in English history. Cumulatively he had some influence on the course of events, even though his contributions often counterbalanced each other. Despite what his contemporaries and subsequent historians have said about him, the final verdict should be that he was not an evil man. He was just guilty of being very modern.

Chapter VI Footnotes

1. The Leveller Richard Overton is, I think, a very close second. See Frank, <u>Levellers</u>, passim.

2. A durable London editor named Samuel Pecke runs Nedham a very close second in this area. See Frank, <u>BN</u>, passim.

3. Firth, <u>Last Years</u>, p. 71.

4. Felix Raab, <u>The English Face of Machiavelli</u>, London: Routledge & Kegan Paul, 1964, pp. 159-163 and 228-230, details Nedham's frequent and varied use of Machiavelli, ranging from citing him as a symbol of conspiratorial villainy to quoting him as a supporter of moderate republicanism. Helpful to an understanding of Nedham's intellectual kinship with Hobbes is Quentin Skinner, "The Ideological Context of Hobbes's Political Thought," <u>Historical Journal</u>, IX (1966), 286-317; and his chapter "Conquest and Consent: Thomas Hobbes and the Engagement Controversy" in Aylmer, <u>The Interregnum</u>, pp. 79-98.

APPENDIX A

A CHRONOLOGY OF THE FRIENDSHIP BETWEEN
NEDHAM AND MILTON

1647: The following item, from Parker, *Milton*, p. 312, is at best inconclusive:

> Some cryptic notes by Samuel Hartlib, probably made at some time in 1647, seem to record his recognition of the end of Milton's experiments in teaching. He wrote: 'Mr. Milton's Academy and Mr. Lawrence's Academy'--and then deleted 'Mr. Milton's'. More provocative are some jottings following a note on 'Sir William Waller's College at Winchester, or Plantation of Hampshire'. One of these is: 'Foundation of an Academy. His removing of Mr. Milton'--with the last four words cancelled. Hartlib also listed some possible 'Commissioners for the Act of the Council for schooling', among them Mr. (John) Dury, Mr. (John?) Pell, Mr. (William?) Rand, Dr. (Thomas?) Horne, (Marchamont) Needham, and Milton. These scribblings tell us more about Hartlib than they do about Milton, and yet hint at the widening circle of Milton's acquaintance.

June 23, 1649: The order of the Council of State "That Mr. Milton do examine the papers of Pragmaticus, and report what he finds in them to the Council." (Masson, *Milton*, IV, 89.)

June 8, 1650: The prospectus for *Mercurius Policus* presented to the Council of State: possibly Milton played a small part in this project.

Jan. 23, 1651 to Jan. 22, 1952: Milton serves as special licenser of <u>Mercurius Politicus</u>. (For details see Masson, <u>Milton</u>, IV, pp. 325-335; Parker, <u>Milton</u>, pp. 993f.; French, "Milton, Needham and 'Politicus'"; and Beller "Milton and 'Mercurius Politicus'," <u>The Huntington Library Quarterly</u>, V (1941-42), 479-487.

1652-1653: Nedham lives near Milton's residence in Petty France in Westminster. (Masson, <u>Milton</u>, IV, 443.)

1652-1660: Masson (<u>Milton</u>, V. pp. 229f.) quotes Milton's elder nephew Edward Phillips that during these years Milton "was frequently visited by persons of quality, particularly my Lady Ranalegh (whose son for some time he instructed), all learned foreigners of note (who could not part out of this city without giving a visit to a person so eminent), and lastly by particular friends that had a high esteem for him: viz. Mr. Andrew Marwell, young Lawrence (the son of him that was President of Oliver's Council),...Mr. Marchamont Needham, the writer of <u>Politicus</u>, and above all Mr. Cyriack Skinner."

1654-1660: June 8, 1654; Nov. 25, 1658; Feb. 27, 1659; Sept. 6, 1659; Oct. 20, 1659; March 8, 1660: advertisements for various of Milton's works appear in <u>Mercurius Politicus</u>. (French, "Milton, Needham, and 'Politicus'," pp. 251f.)

Nov. 23, 1658: Milton and Nedham walk in the same group in Cromwell's funeral procession. (French, <u>Life Records</u>, IV, 245; Hill, <u>Milton</u>, p. 213.)

Nov. 1659: Milton and Nedham each inherit ₤10 Bradshaw's will.

1660-1674: Masson (<u>Milton</u>, VI, 452) speculates that Nedham's visits to Milton were now "very rare." Hill (<u>Milton</u>, p. 214) merely says that after the Restoration Milton's "association with Marvell and Nedham continued."

Dec. 23, 1674: Sir Peter Wentworth leaves "his worthy and very learned Friend" John Milton ₤100, and among many other legacies ₤50 to Mr. or Dr. Needham. (French, <u>Life Records</u>, V, 64.)

Note: I am omitting from the above "evidence" literally dozens of attacks, starting in 1645 and rising to a crescendo in 1660, which link Milton and Nedham together as traitors, subversives, radicals, liars, etc. Despite such linkage, and despite their long acquaintanceship, I can find no evidence that Nedham influenced Milton or vice versa. Both could write "Miltonic" sentences; both were stylistically versatile. The fact that during the 1650's they often agreed on the state of the nation does not imply the influence of one on the other. Both men were politically shrewd, and Milton, while not as fluid as Nedham, was not frozen into any one political stance. Milton was, of course, more devout than Nedham, but he too had a sense of humor, one often directed against the clergy and even, on occasion, against various theological sacred cows. Thus I see these two men as intermittent friends who apparently enjoyed each other's company, but I very much doubt if either was at all heavily in intellectual debt to the other.

APPENDIX B

The Relationship between <u>Mercurius Politicus</u> and <u>The Case of the Commonwealth of England, Stated</u> and <u>The Excellencie Of A Free State</u>.

The initials after each entry refer to my sources, which are corroborated by my own research:

    F = French, J. Milton, "Milton, Needham, and 'Mercurius Politicus'," <u>Studies in Philology</u>, XXXIII (1936), 236-252.

    B = Beller, Elmer A., "Milton and 'Mercurius Politicus'," <u>The Huntington Library Quarterly</u>, V (1941-42), 479-487.

    A = Anthony, H. Sylvia, "Mercurius Politicus Under Milton," <u>Journal of the History of Ideas</u>, XXVII (1966), 593-609.

Mercurius Politicus number and date	The Case (1st ed.) page numbers	
16	9/19-26 <u>1650</u>	17-19	F
17	9/26-10/3	19-21	F
18	10/3-10	21	F
19	10/10-17	21	F
20	10/17-24	22-24	F
21	10/24-31	23-24	F
22	10/31-11/7	30-35	F
23	11/7-14	18-19	F
24	11/14-21	14-15	F
25	11/21-28	15-16	F
26	11/28-12/5	6-9	F
27	12/5-12	104-105 (2nd ed.): Salmasius F	
28	12/12-19	106-107 (2nd ed.): Salmasius F	
29	12/19-26	107-108 105 (2nd ed.): Salmasius F	
30	12/26/1/2 <u>1651</u>	attack on Levellers--not reprinted B	

31	1/2-9		108 (2nd ed.): Hobbes F
32	1/9-16		108-109 (2nd ed.): Hobbes F
33	1/16-23		109 (2nd ed.): Hobbes F
34	1/23-30		110-111 (2nd ed.): Hobbes F
35	1/30-2/6		82 B
36	2/6-13		extracted in *Excellencie* A
37	2/13-20		extracted in *Excellencie* p. 20 F,B,A
38	2/20-27		40-41 F
39	2/27-3/6		43-44 F
40	3/6-13		44-45, 65 F
41	3/13-20		45-46 F
42	3/20-27		93 B
43	3/27-4/3		57 F
44	4/3-10	a series	(attack on Scots--not (reprinted B
45	4/10-17		(64-65 F
46	4/17-24	of	(58 F
47	4/24-5/1		(attack on Scots--not (reprinted B
48	5/1-8	anti-Scot	(52-53 F
49	5/8-15		(attack on Scots--not (reprinted B
50	5/15-22		(attack on Scots--not (reprinted B
51	5/22-29	editorials	(attack on Scots--not
52	5/29-6/5		(reprinted B
53	6/5-12		14-15 F
54	6/12-19		(62-63 a series of
55	6/19-26		(anti-
56	6/26-7/3		(Presbyterian
57	7/3-10		(editorials,
58	7/10-17		(of which
59	7/17-24		(only the first
60	7/31-8/7		(is reprinted in
61	7/31-8/7		(*The Case* B

62	8/7-14		64-65 B
63	8/14-21		82 B
64	8/21-28		(from The True
			(Portraiture of Kings
65	8/28-9/4		(of England (1650),
			(pp. 17-38 - not by
			(Nedham. Part of no.
			(64 is extracted in
			(Excellencie A
66	9/4-11		(Two editorials at-
			(tacking the enemies
			(of the Commonwealth
67	9/11-18		(and bragging that its
			(victories show God's
			(approval. No. 66 is
			(reprinted at the end
			(of this Appendix.
68	9/18-25		83-85 F reprinted in Excellencie F,A
69	9/25-10/2		80-82 F

The Excellencie Of A Free State

Page numbers

70	10/2-9		13-17 F
71	10/9-16		1-4 F
72	10/16-23		8-13 F
73	10/23-30		5-8 F
74	10/30-11/6		242-246 (These are the concluding pages of Excellencie.)
75	11/6-13		
76	11/13-20		From Thomas May's 'Lucan' F
77	11/20-27		23-27 F
78	11/27-12/4		27-28 F
79	12/4-11		28-32 F
80	12/11-18		32-35 F
81	12/18-25		35-39 F
82	12/25-1/1	1652	39-44 F
83	1/1-8		44-49 F
84	1/8-15		49-53 F
85	1/15-22		54-58 F

86	1/22-29	58-64	F
87	1/29-2/5	64-71	F
88	2/5-12	71/75	
89	2/12-19		
90	2/19-26	———	
91	2/26-3/4	75-80	F
92	3/4-11	81-93	F
93	3/11-18	93-98	F
94	3/18-25	98-103	F
95	3/25-4/1	103-111	F
96	4/1-8	111-119	F)Plus an-
		119-127	F)nouncements
97	4/8-15	129-136	F)that this
98	4/15-22	145-152	)entire edi-

torial series, nos.

99	4/22-29	70-114, is to be pub-	
		lished as a book. A	
100	4/29-5/6	152-160	F
101	5/6-13	160-167	F
102	5/13-20	167-173	F
103	5/20-27	173-178	F
104	5/27-6/3	178-184	F Plus an

extract from <u>The Case</u>
A

105	6/3-10	184-192	F
106	6/10-17	192-199	F
107	6/17-24	199-204	F
108	6/24-7/1	204-212	F
109	7/1-8	212-220	F
110	7/8-15	220-227	F
111	7/15-22	228-231	F
112	7/22-29	231-234	F
113	7/29-8/5	234-242	F
114	8/5-12		

This final editorial consists largely of further selections from a sermon preached by Peter Sterry on November 5, 1651, with a brief introduction and conclusion by Nedham. Parts of the sermon appear in <u>Excellencie</u>. See also no. 74, above.   A

Breakdown by subject of certain editorials from The Excellencie in Mercurius Politicus; from J.G.A. Pocock, The Machiavellian Moment, Princeton: Princeton University Press, 1975, pp. 382f.

Anti-Presbyterian   nos. 99, 114
Pro-greater democracy in Scotland nos. 65, 73
Pro-arms in the hands of the people no. 103
Pro-rotation in office   nos. 72, 74, 78, 79, 87,
                              91, 92, 100
Anti-hereditary aristocracies   nos. 70, 72, 73,
                              84, 86, 89
Support of the Roman Republic, and of Athens over Sparta   nos. 71, 73, 84, 88, 91
Anti-Venice as an aristocracy   nos. 70, 73, 84.

Editorial from Mercurius Politicus, no. 66, Sept. 4-11, 1651.

If after so many eminent discoveries of the will and purpose of God touching the establishment of this Commonwealth any man shall yet be so much of a sot as to continue a malignant, let him remember how God useth to dipose of his incorrigible and implacable enemies. But I perceive one main impediment that keeps men form quitting their old corrupt principles is the fear of being counted a Turncoat. Yet, know that, if God once declare, as it were from Heaven, against thy ways, thy principles, or thy party, then it is no dishonour, but ingenuity and thy duty, to turn: for He hath said in this case (Ps. vii. 12-13), If a man do not turn, He will whet his sword; He hath bent his bow and made it ready; He hath prepared for him the instruments of death and destruction.

It was a loud declaration from Heaven at Naseby, when by a despised company it pleased God to decide the controversy, and also in the year 1647, when God owned the cause against a powerful faction both in Parliament and City. But in the year 1648 He spake louder in the midst of those alarms and insurrections, when by a small handful He overthrew Hamilton's numerous proud army in Lancashire, resettled the whole nation, and brought the King to the bar and block of Justice. Remember how eminently He hath appeared since, both in Ireland and Scotland, by many miraculous successes; but especially at Dunbar, where by a wearied and sick handful of men, cooped in a nook of land within the arms of the sea and encompassed with extreme disadvantages, He was pleased so visibly to make bare His own arm, and give a total rout to that numerous Scottish army in their own country, where, being well accomplished and provided both with numbers and Necessaries, they reckoned themselves sure of spoil and victory. In all these particulars, and many others since, God did sufficiently signify His own will and pleasure; but His loudest declaration of all was mightily set forth in the late sudden revolutions and actions before and at Worcester, whereby He unquestionably appears to have given a full and final decision of the controversy, and seems as it were with His own finger to point out to all the world His resolutions for England.

For the better clearing of this, let every man examine his own heart, and enter into a few serious considerations. First, consider the power of the Enemy, being a very formidable body and well provided, and having their spirits double-edged with revenge and despair, the strongest ingredients of resolution.

Consider likewise the policy of the Enemy, that for the present laid aside all spleen against any one party, that he might the better make use of all parties, so that his army was a medley of all interests, a combination of men of all opinions. The rough Cavalier and the round Presbyterian were made to square together under a disguise of the Covenant, to draw in, if it were possible, almost the whole nation; whom they believed (and made foreign nations also believe they would be) ready to rise as one man for their assistance.

Next consider the Enemy's hope of success, having gotten the start of our army, so as to march into the very heart of the land before they were were put to any considerable stand, and at such a time as the militias in most counties were unsettled. Yet it pleased God they afterwards acted and proceeded with such alacrity that they immediately raised new forces in all parts: wherein it is very remarkable how willingly they marched to the main army, having a month's advance, and how bravely they fought, despatching their own work with good will and courage, so as to be able to return home again within the month.

Consider the several links in this great chain of mercies: as first the notable success of Major General Lambert at our first landing in Fife; next our taking Saint Johnston [Perth], and the enemy's march into England, which (as God in his wisdom ordered it) was a great mercy, it proving the only means of shorning that tedious expensive war; after this, the taking of Stirling Castle, bragged by the Scots to be unconquerable; then that most seasonable mercy of [Robert] Lilburne's routing the Earl of Derby's body, which might have grown up to another army; as also the surprising of the great Scotch lords, lairds, and their prime boutefeus of the priesthood, who were kindling coals in Scotland; but above all that glorious day of decision at Worcester, followed since with the taking of Dundee, and other considerable passages which render the Scots' interest expiring in their own country. Add, to the sweetening of all these mercies, the little blood we have lost. Nor must it be forgotten what experiences we had in the appearances and alacrity of the London regiments, whose gallantry appeared, as in many other ways, so especially in this, that they had Young Tarquin's Declaration burnt at the heads of their regiments.

Take two or three considerations more, and then we have done. Let the old Malignants and Cavaliers consider that, in what shape soever they have appeared, with what pretences soever they have clothed their confederacies, yet God hath found them out and confounded them. Let the New Malignants of the Presbyterian opinion consider how often and notoriously God hath checked them, and cursed their unrighteous combination with the Old Malignants. Let both Old and New consider what an inseparable curse is annexed (as I have often told you) to the family and interest of the Tarquins, that it proves ruin and destruction to all that own it. Let England herself and all the nations about consider what God hath done for England, and how in this auspicious time of trial He gave in the hearts of the people to live and die for the present Government. Lastly, let all parties consider it is high time to lay aside animosities and unite again upon the common interests of our nation; and there is no doubt that the Parliament will consider that, as God hath His design of glory in all these things, so it should be their design to improve them all to that end, and for the ease and benefit of so willing and obedient a people. (Masson, *Milton*, IV, 332-334.)

BIBLIOGRAPHY

Note: For my own intellectual background in writing this book the reader is referred to the Bibliographies in The Levellers and The Beginnings of the English Newspaper. What follows are only those works mentioned in the text and footnotes of Cromwell's Press Agent.

I. BOOKS AND PAMPHLETS PRINTED BEFORE 1700

(Unless otherwise noted, the place of publication is London.)

Anti-Machiavell, or Honesty against Policy, 1647.

Bolnest, Edward, Medicina Instaurata, 1665.

Burnet, Gilbert, The Memories of the Lives and Actions of James and William, Dukes of Hamilton, 1677.

Castle, George, The Chymical Galenist, 1667.

Character of the Rump, The, 1660.

Cheynell, Francis (?), Aulicus, his Hue and Cry Sent forth after Britanicus, 1645.

Cleveland, John, The Character of a London Diural, Oxford, 1645.

Cleveland, John (?), True Character of a Rigid Presbyter, The, 1645.

Committee-Mans Complaint, and the Scots Honest Usage, The, 1647.

Dialogue between Thomas Scot and Marchamont Nedham, A., 1660.

Downfall of Mercurius Britanicus/Pragmaticus/Politicus, The, 1660.

Dryden, John, Absalom and Achitophel, 1681.

E., J., *A Narrative of the cause and manner of the Imprisonment of the Lords*, 1677.

Edwards, Thomas, *Gangraena*, 1646.

Evelyn, John, *The Late News...from Bruxels Unmasked*, 1660.

F., R. *Mercrius Heliconicus*, 1651.
Mercurius Heliconicus, Numb. 2, 1651.
Radius Heliconicus, 1651.

Fell, John, *The Interest of England Stated*, 1659.

Ferguson, Robert, *No Protestant Plot*, 1681.
The Third Part of No Protestant Plot, 1682.

Goodwin, John, *The Triers Tried*, 1657.
Triumviri, 1658.

Harrington, James, *The Commonwealth of Oceana*, 1656.

Heath, James, *A Brief Chronicle of the late Intestine War*, "The Second Impression greatly enlarged," 1663.

Hobbes, Thomas, *De Corpore Politico*, 1650.

Holles, Denzil, *The Long Parliament Dissolved*, 1676.
Some Consideration Upon the Question, Whether the Parliament is dissolved, 1676.

Howell, James, *Some Sober Inspections Made into the Late-long Parliament*, 1655.

[Ireton, Henry], *The Remonstrance of the Army*, 1648.

Kilbourne, W., *A New-Years-Gift For Mercurius Politicus*, 1660.

L'Estrange, Roger, *L'Estrange His Apology*, 1660.

Letter from a Person of Quality, A., 1676.

Lier laid open, The, 1648.

Lilburne, John, An Answer to Nine Arguments, 1638, 1645.
As You Were, Amsterdam (?), 1652.
Copie of a Letter...To Mr. William Prinne, A., 1645.

London Printer His Lamentation, The, 1660.

Marten, Henry, The Independency of England, 1648.

"Mercurius Melancholicus," Mistris Parliament, 1648
Craftie Cromwell, 1648.

Milton, John, Areopagitica, 1644.
Defensio pro Populo Anglicano, 1651.
Defensio Secunda, 1654.
The Ready and Easy Way, 1660.

Nedham, Marchamont, See Section III of this Bibliography.

O. Cromwell's Thanks to the Lord Generall... Together with an Hue and Cry after Mercurius Politicus.

P., H., Seasonable Question and an Useful Answer, A, 1676.

Poore Committee-Mans Accompt, The, 1647.

Prynne, William, A Brief, Necessary Vindication of the Old and New Secluded Members, 1659.
A Checke to Britannicus, 1644.
IX Queries, 1647.
A True and Perfect Narrative, 1659.
Truth Triumphing over Falsehood, Antiquity over Novelty, 1645.

Rogers, Nathaniel, A Letter discovering the cause of Gods continuing Wrath against the Nation, 1643.

Rope for Pol, A, 1660.

Saumaise, Claude (Salmasius), Defensio Regia, 1649.

Second Character of Mercurius Politicus, The, 1650.

Sprackling, Robert, Medala Ignorantiae, 1665.

Sylvius, Franciscus De Le Boë, A New Idea of the Practise of Physic, 1675.

Taylor, John ("The Water Poet"), Mercurius Aquaticus, 1644.
Rebels Anathematized and Anatomized, 1645.

Treason Arraigned, 1660.

True Character of Mercurius Aulicus, The, 1645.

True Catalogue, Or An Account of the Several Places and most Eminent Persons, A, 1659.

Twysden, John, Medicina Veterum Vindicata, 1666.

Vernon, George, The Life of ...Peter Heylyn, 1682.

Vicars, John, The Schismatick Sifted, 1646.

Wharton, George, A Second Narrative of the Late Parliament (so called), 1659.

Wither, George, The Great Assises Holden in in Parnassus, 1645.

Wood, Anthony á., Athenae Oxoniensis, 1691.

Wortley, Francis, Characters and Elegies, 1646.
Mercurius Britanicus His Welcome to Hell: With the Devils Blessing, 1647.

II. INTERREGNUM NEWSPAPERS

The Kingdomes Weekly Intelligencer

The Man in the Moon

Mercurius Academicus

Mercurius Anti-Britanicus

Mercurius Aulicus

Mercurius Bellicus

Mercurius Britanicus - Nedham

Mercurius Elencticus

Mercurius Melancholicus

Mercurius Politicus - Nedham

Mercurius Pragmaticus - Nedham

Mercurius Pragmaticus (For King Charles II) - Nedham

Mercurius Pragmaticus (For King Charls II)

Mercurius Pragmaticus, For King Charls II

Mercurius Pragmaticus, Revived

The Moderate Informer - Nedham

Perfect Occurrences

The Publick Intelligencer - Nedham

III. MARCHAMONT NEDHAM

This list is chronological. The short title is followed by the author's name or nom de plume, when given; next the date, then, in parentheses, the printer, when given, and the number of pages; and last, the citation of those who attribute the work to Nedham: Wing (<u>Short Title Catalogue</u>), Wood ("Nedham" in <u>Athenae Oxoniensis</u>), Firth ("Nedham" in <u>The Dictionary of National Biography</u>), Th. (<u>Catalogue of the Thomason Tracts</u>). In every case the place of publication is London.

<u>A Check to the Checker of Britanicus</u>, 1644. (Printed by Andrew Coe; 30 pp.) Wing, Wood, Firth, Th.

'To the Reader' - signed M. N. - In Lilburne, <u>An Answer to Nine Arguments</u>, 1644. (No printer given; Nedham's contribution is 2 pp.).

[Mercurius Britanicus, <u>His Apologie to All Well-affected People</u>, 1645. Probably by Thomas Audley, possibly by Nedham.]

<u>Independencie No Schisme</u> - "By M. N. Med. Pr." - 1646. (Printed by Robert White; 12 pp.) Wing, Firth, Th.

<u>The Case of the Kingdom Stated</u>, 1647 - 3 eds., all in 1647. (No printer given; 18 pp.) Wing, Wood, Firth, Th.

<u>The Lawyer of Lincolnes-Inne Reformed</u> - "By the Author of the Case of the Kingdome, &c." - 1647. (No printer given; 12 pp.) Wing, Firth, Th.

<u>The Levellers levell'd</u> - "By Mercurius Pragmaticus" - 1647. (No printer given; 16 pp.) Wing, Wood, Firth, Th.

<u>Loyalty speakes Truth</u>, 1648. (No printer given; 8 pp.) Wing.

An Answer to a Declaration of the Lords and Commons - "By Mercurius Pragmaticus" - 1648. (Printed for J.S.; 13 pp.) Wing.

The Solemn League and Covenant - signed at end "Ma. Nedham" - 1648. (No printer given; 2 pp.) Wing.

The Manifold Practises and Attempts of the Hamiltons, 1648. (No printer given; 23 pp.) Wing, Wood, Firth, Th.

The Reverend Alderman Atkins (The Shit Breech) His Speech - "By Mercurius Pragmaticus" - 1648. (No printer given; 6 pp.)

A Plea for the King and Kingdome - "By Mercurius Pragmaticus" - 1648. (No printer given; 28 pp.) Wing, Wood, Firth, Th.

Digitus Dei, 1649. (No printer given; 31 pp.) Wing, Wood, Firth, Th.

A Most Pithy Exhortation - "By Mercurius Pragmaticus" - 1649. (No printer given; 6 pp.) Wing.

Certain Considerations - "By Marchamont Nedham, Gent." - 1649. (No printer given; 14 pp.) Wing.

The Case of the Commonwealth of the England, Stated - "By Marchamont Nedham, Gent." - 2 eds., 1650. (Both eds. printed for E. Blackmore and R. Lowndes; the first ca. 100 pp., the second 111 pp.) Wing, Wood, Firth, Th.

Of the Dominion, or Ownership of the Sea: John Selden's 'Mare Clausum,' "Translated into English, and set forth with some additional Evidences and Discourses, by Marchamont Nedham," 1652. (Printed by William Du-Gard; 537 pp.) Wing, Wood, Firth.

[Almost certainly not by Nedham: A True Case of the State of the Commonwealth, 1654.]

The Excellencie Of A Free State, 1656. (Printed for Thomas Brewster; 246 pp.) Wing, Wood, Firth, Th. (The edition sent to America in the late eighteenth century was entitled The Right Constitution of a Commonwealth.)

The Great Accuser Cast Down - "By Marchamont Nedham, Gent." - 1657. (Printed by Tho. Newcomb, for George Sawbridge; 150 pp.) Wing, Wood, Firth, Th.

Interest will not Lie - "By Mar. Nedham" - 1659. (Printed by Tho. Newcomb; 55 pp.) Wing, Wood, Firth, Th.

Newes from Brussels, 1660. (No printer given; 8 pp.) Wing, Wood, Firth, Th.

The Cities Feast to the Lord Protector - "By Marchemount Needham" - 1661 (Printed for Henry Marsh; 1 p.) Wing.

A Short History of the English Rebellion - "By Marchamont Nedham" - 1661. (No printer given; 37 pp.) Wing, Wood, Firth. Two other eds. of A Short History appeared in 1661, both attached to 'The True Character of a Rigid Presbyter.'

A Discourse Concerning Schools and School-Masters "By M.N." - 1663. (Printed for H.H.; 16 pp.) Wing, Wood, Firth.

Medala Medicinae - "By M. N. Med. Londineus" - (Printed by Richard Lownds; 516 pp.) Wing, Wood, Firth.

Preface to Edward Bolnest, 'Medicina Instaurata,' 1665: An Epistolary Discourse upon the whole, by the Author of Medala Medicinae, signed. Mar. Nedham. (Printed for John Starkey; Nedham's Preface is 24 pp.) Wood, Firth.

A Preface written by Dr. Mar. Nedham to Franciscus De Le Boë, Sylvius, 'A New Idea of the Practise of Physic,' (Printed for B. Aylmer; Nedham's Preface is 19 pp.) Wing, Wood, Firth.

A Pacquet of Advice and Animadversions, 2 eds. (No printer given; the first ed. is 74 pp., the second, in smaller type, ca. 50 pp.) Wing, Wood, Firth.

A Second Pacquet of Advices, 1677. (Sold By Jonathan Edwin; 76 pp.) Wing, Wood, Firth.

Honesty's best Policy, 1678. (No printer given; 18 pp.) Wing.

The Pacquet-Boat Advice, 1678. (No printer given; 21 pp.) Wing.

Christianissimus Christianandus, 1678. (Two eds. appeared in 1678, both printed by Henry Hills for Jonathan Edwin; 80 pp. It was also promptly translated into German and French.) Wing, Wood, Firth.

IV. BOOKS AND ARTICLES PRINTED AFTER 1700

Abbot, Wilbur C., The Writings and Speeches of Oliver Cromwell, Cambridge: Harvard University Press, 1937-1947.

Anthony, H. Sylvia, "Mercurius Politicus Under Milton," Journal of the History of Ideas, XXVII (1966), 593-609.

Aylmer, G. E., ed., The Interregnum: The Quest for Settlement 1640-1660, London: Macmillan, 1972.

Beller, Elmer A., "Milton and 'Mercurius Politicus'," The Huntington Library Quarterly, V (1941-42), 479-487.

Brailsford, H. N., *The Levellers and the English Revolution*, London: The Cresset Press, 1961.

Calendar of State Papers, Domestic.

Clark, G. N., *The Later Stuarts 1660-1714*, Oxford: At the Clarendon Press, 1947.

Cleveland, John, *The Poems of John Cleveland*, ed. Brian Morris and Eleanor Withington, Oxford: At the Clarendon Press, 1967.

Clyde, William M., *The Struggle for the Freedom of the Press from Caxton to Cromwell*, reprinted New York: Burt Franklin, 1970.

Creighton, Mandell, "Peter Heylyn" in *The Dictionary of National Biography*.

Davies, Godfrey, *The Restoration of Charles II, 1658-1660*, San Marino: The Huntington Library, 1955.

Draper, F. W. M., *Four Centuries of Merchant Taylors' School 1561-1961*, London: Oxford University Press, 1962.

Dryden, John, *The Works of John Dryden*, Vol. I, ed. Edward Niles and H. T. Swedenberg, Jr., Berkeley: University of California Press, 1956.

Firth, Charles, Harding, *The Last Days of the Protectorate*, London: Longmans, Green, and Co., 1909.
"Marchamont Nedham" in *The Dictionary of National Biography*.
"Peter Wentworth" in *The Dictionary of National Biography*.

Frank, Joseph, <u>The Beginnings of the English Newspaper</u>, Cambridge: Harvard University Press, 1961.
<u>Hobbled Pegasus</u>, Albuquerque: University of New Mexico Press, 1968.
<u>The Levellers</u>, Cambridge: Harvard University Press, 1955.

French, J. Milton, <u>The Life Records of John Milton</u>, New Brunswick: Rutgers University Press, 1949-1958.
"Milton, Needham, and 'Mercurius Politicus'," <u>Studies in Philology</u>, XXVI (1936), 236-252.

Gardiner, Samuel Rawson, <u>History of England From the Accession of James I To the Outbreak of the Civil War</u>, London: Longmans, Green, and Co., 1895.
<u>History of the Commonwealth and Protectorate</u>, London: Longmans, Green, and Co., 1903.
<u>History of the Great Civil War</u>, London: Longmans, Green, and Co., 1893-1898.

Gordon, Alexander, "John Goodwin" in <u>The Dictionary of National Biography</u>.

Green, V.H.H., <u>A History of Oxford</u>, London: P.T. Botsford, Ltd., 1974.

Gretton, Mary Sturge, <u>Burford Past and Present</u>, London: Faber and Faber Limited, 1945.

Gretton, R.H., <u>The Burford Records</u>, Oxford: At the Clarendon Press, 1920.

Haley, K.H.D., *The First Earl of Shaftesbury*, Oxford: Clarendon Press, 1968.

Hanbury, Benjamin, ed., *Historical Memorials Relating to the Independents*, London: Printed for the Congregational Union of England and Wales, 1839-44.

Hexter, J.H. *The Reign of King Pym*, Cambridge: Harvard University Press, 1941.

Hill, Christopher, *The Century of Revolution*, Edinburgh: Thomas Nelson and Sons, Ltd., 1961.
Change and Continuity in Seventeenth-Century England, London: Weidenfeld and Nicolson, 1974.
God's Englishman: Oliver Cromwell and the English Revolution, New York: The Dial Press, 1970.
Milton and the English Revolution, New York: The Viking Press, 1977.
The World Turned Upside Down, London: Temple Smith, 1972.

Historical Manuscripts Commission: Fourth Report, Fifth Report.

Hutchinson, Lucy, *Memoirs of the Life of Colonel Hutchinson*, London: J.M. Dent and Sons, 1908.

Inglis, Brian, *A History of Medicine*, London: Weidenfeld and Nicolson, 1965.

Jackson, Thomas, *The Life of John Goodwin*, London: Longmans, Green, Reeder, and Dyer, 1872.

Jessup, Mary, *A History of Oxfordshire*, London: Chichester, Phillmore & Co., Ltd., 1975.

Journal of the House of Lords.

Keynes, Geoffrey, *John Evelyn*, New York: The Grolier Club, 1937.

King, Lester, *The Road to Medical Enlightenment, 1650-1695*, London: Macdonald, 1970.

Knachel, Philip, ed., *The Case of the Commonwealth of England, Stated, by Marchamont Nedham*, Washington, D.C.: The Folger Shakespeare Library, 1969.

Koestler, Arthur, *Arrow in the Blue*, London: Collins, 1952.
Darkness at Noon, New York: Macmillan, 1941.

Mallet, Charles, *A History of the University of Oxford*, New York: Longmans, Green and Co., 1924.

Masson, David, *The Life of John Milton*, reprinted New York: Peter Smith, 1946.

Muddiman, J.G., *The King's Journalist 1659-1689*, London: John Lane The Bodley Head Limited, 1923.

Newton, Arthur Percival, *The Colonising Activities of the English Puritans*, reprinted Port Washington, N.Y.: Kennikat Press, Inc., 1966.

O'Malley, C.D., ed., *The History of Medical Education*, Berkeley: University of California Press, 1970.

Parker, William Riley, *Milton - A Biography*, Oxford: At the Clarendon Press, 1968.

Pearl, Valerie, *London and the Outbreak of the Puritan Revolution*, Oxford: Oxford University Press, 1961.

Pinto, Vivian de Sola, Enthusiast in Wit, A Portrait of John Wilmot Earl of Rochester, 1647-1680, London: Routledge & Kegan Paul, 1962.

Pocock, J. G. A., The Machiavellian Moment, Princeton: Princeton University Press, 1975.

Raab, Felix, The English Face of Machiavelli, London: Routledge & Kegan Paul, 1964.

Roots, Ivan, Commonwealth and Protectorate: The English Civil War and Its Aftermath, New York: Schocken Books, 1966.

Rubinstein, Hilary L., Captain Luckless: James, First Duke of Hamilton 1606-1649, Edinburgh: Scottish Academic Press, 1975.

Rushworth, John, Historical Collections, The Second Edition, London: D. Browne, 1721-22.

Shaw, Peter, The Character of John Adams, New York: W. W. Norton and Company, Inc., 1977.

Skinner, Quentin, "The Ideological Context of Hobbes's Political Thought," Historical Journal, IX (1966), 286-317.

Snow, Vernon F., Essex the Rebel, Lincoln: University of Nebraska Press, 1970.

Stearns, Raymond Phineas, The Strenuous Puritan: Hugh Peter 1598-1660, Urbana: University of Illinois Press, 1954.

Thomas, P. W., Sir John Berkenhead 1617-1679: A Royalist Career in Politics and Polemics, Oxford: At the Clarendon Press, 1969.

[Thomason], *Catalogue of the Pamphlets, Books, Newspapers, and Manuscripts Relating to the Civil War, the Commonwealth, and Restoration, Collected by George Thomason, 1640-1661*, London: The British Museum, 1908.

Thurloe, John, *A Collection of the State Papers of John Thurloe*, ed. Thomas Birch, London: F. Gyles, 1742.

Underdown, David, *Pride's Purge: Politics in the Puritan Revolution*, Oxford: At the Clarendon Press, 1971.
Royalist Conspiracy in England 1649-1660, New Haven: Yale University Press, 1960.

Varley, Frederick J., *Mercurius Aulicus*, Oxford: Basil Blackwell, 1948.

Wallace, John M., *Destiny His Choice: The Loyalism of Andrew Marvell*, Cambridge: At the University Press, 1968.

Wedgwood, C. V., *The Thirty Years War*, London: Jonathan Cape, 1938.

Whitelock, Bulstrode, *Memorials of English Affairs*, Oxford: At the University Press, 1853.

Wing, Donald, *A Gallery of Ghosts*, New York: Modern Language Association, 1967.
Short-Title Catalogue....1641-1700, New York: Columbia University Press, 1945-1951.